Bitcoin Prophecy

ARIEL A. AGUILAR

For future reference, the initial price of this book in June 2024 was €25 or 46,275 satoshis.

If you want to know more about Bitcoin visit:

www.arielaguilar.com

ISBN 9798343649123 (Paperback)
ISBN 9798343652222 (Hardcover)

Front cover image by *Leoraam*.
Book design by *Leoraam*.

First printing edition 2024.

To my father Alberto,

Who inspired in me the love for freedom.

Contents

i

SECTION TWO

What is Bitcoin?

iv

SECTION THREE
Politics, Economics and Philosophy

Bitcoin Future

The Spiritual

Preface

This book is truly inspiring, offering a bit of everything: it might ruffle some feathers, but it also has the power to motivate. It provides a clear and straightforward guide to understanding Argentina's intricate economic history, the concept of Bitcoin, its principles, functionality, and the potential impact on our lives.

I will go through economics, politics, philosophy, history, religion, cryptography, game theory, the rational and the mystical.

The book is divided into five sections:

- **Argentina**

- **What Bitcoin Is**

- **Money, Politics and Economics**

- **Bitcoin Future**

- **The Spiritual**

You may ask: What does Argentina's history has anything to do with Bitcoin? I've chosen to include what I've personally experienced and learned about my country's past after witnessing the incredulous expressions on foreigners faces when I recount our history to them. They cannot believe what they are hearing. Argentina mirrors the narrative repeated all throughout world history, embodying the archetype of rising from nothing, scaling to the peaks of global prominence, only to plummet into the depths of despair, and then emerging anew. It's a cyclic journey, fraught with highs and lows, offering profound economic insights for those willing to learn from its tumultuous past and precious lessons.

You may ask why Bitcoin? How does it solve my economic problems and those of the world economy? Isn't it old technology to be replaced by newer blockchains? 'Bitcoin is too complicated, I will never understand it'.

In this book you will learn Bitcoin's core principles in an easy to understand manner and you will learn how Bitcoin is revolutionary and fits in the larger picture of the coming world's economy. You will also learn to read the economic signals to see if your country is doing 'Argentina things' and how we argentines manage to survive and circumvent them. You will learn why you need to start saving in Bitcoin today and why and how it will affect the course of your life and that of your loved ones.

Lastly, I hope this book sparks new insights and a deeper understanding in you.

Enjoy!

Ariel A. Aguilar

August 2024

1. Argentina

Argentina, the land of silver.
Oh, my beautiful country.

1.1 ARGENTINA'S BIRTH

Since the arrival of the first conquistadores to this beautiful land, tales have abounded of a river flowing with silver (Rio de la Plata), promising untold fortunes to those who ventured forth. Just as there were explorers seeking *El Dorado* in the north, there were also adventurers in search of a *land of abundance* with silver in the south.

At first, my country was very desolate, savage, and poor. We declared our independence from the Spanish crown in 1816, and chaos ensued for the next foreseeable years. Wars were waged between Unitarians and Federalists, representing a struggle over the degree of centralization or decentralization Argentina should have. Native populations and "barbarians" were looting the interior, while over 90% of the population remained illiterate, unable to read or write.

Fortunately for Argentina, we were blessed with a generation of superb intellectual men known as the *Generation of '37*, that crafted the Constitution that was adopted in 1853. Led by Juan Bautista Alberdi, a free market advocate, it was the first constitution in the world that declared private property as an inalienable human right. It also declared that all foreigners had the same rights as citizens and the preamble of the constitution reads: …"to promote the general welfare and secure the blessings of liberty to ourselves, to our posterity, and to all men of the world who wish to dwell on argentine soil"… thus opening its doors to whoever wanted to be a free man and inhabit its land.

From its origins as a nation characterized by widespread illiteracy, perceived savagery, and abject poverty, Argentina, alongside the USA, became a beacon of freedom and hope, attracting millions of people from Europe. By 1880, Argentina was on its way to becoming a world superpower, with the British investing heavily in the construction of an extensive territorial railway network, creating one of the most extensive systems of its time to connect all regions of the eighth largest country in the world. Argentina became one of the world's largest meat producers, with the highest per capita beef consumption on the planet. By 1910, Argentina had risen to become one of the world's top seven economies, even amidst the arrival of millions of impoverished European immigrants seeking refuge from their countries of origin. Applying capitalism and a very small state, with low taxation, the fledgling country had made significant advances not only in economic terms, but also in diverse fields such as literature, science and diplomacy. The phrase 'as rich as an Argentine' became part of world parlance, implying that one could hardly be as rich as an Argentine. Around the extensive lands, palaces and large estates called Estancias were built. With a marked European aesthetic, English train stations, and Paris-like buildings, monuments and parks still remind us today of the greatness that this country reached in its heyday.

Sadly, to Argentina's demise, these groups of immigrants brought with them the socialist, communist, and anarcho-communist ideas popular in Europe. Those ideas ran counter to the free market principles of the framers of the constitution. Gradually, these ideas infiltrated the culture, the media, the education system and the government. The free market ideals of the original constitution were ditched in favor of the new 'democratic', populist ideas of social rights.

Since Argentina offers 'free' (funded by inflation and taxpayers) education at elementary, high school, college, and doctoral levels, any resident or foreigner can study in Argentina *without paying tuition,* even to this day. But there is a catch: the state makes sure to indoctrinate the population on socialist ideals. Aspiring students at the University of Buenos Aires have to go through a propaganda-based introductory year where the state is revered as the savior, and capitalism and businessmen are demonized. In this sense, most of the country is synchronized with these ideas since they hear them from kindergarten, in TV shows, in newspapers, in political discourse...

As we will see in later sections, this has started to change for some part of the population thanks to the work of the libertarians of

4

Argentina with the most recognition by our current president, Javier Milei.

1.2 THE FIRST MILITARY COUPS AND CENTRAL BANK

In 1930, Constitutional Argentina had it's first military coup and the succession of democratic presidents that had been running since 1853 came to an end. It was a chaotic time since branches of the military even started to make coups to other branches of the military. These new 'presidents' would sometimes last months or even days. During these tumultuous times is when two central destructive forces were implemented in 1935: The Central Bank of the Argentine Republic (BCRA) and the income tax. Just as it happened in the United States where both the Central Bank, the Federal Reserve and the income tax were stablished at the same time, so too, it happened in Argentina. Coincidence? I don't think so.

This income tax was imposed on the public as 'a temporary measure' with a provision in the law for it to only last 10 years. It has been renewed ever since, every ten years. Seems nothing is as permanent as a temporary tax.

1.3 GENERAL PERON AND EVITA

General Perón is a pivotal figure in Argentine history, so influential that the 'Peronist movement' endures, with the Peronist Party, i.e., the Justicialist Party, remaining a dominant political force. Some even humorously dub Argentina as 'Peronistan'.

Juan Domingo Perón rose through the ranks of the military GOU (Group of United Officers), orchestrating coups and edging ever closer to power. His studies in Italy during the 1930s brought him face-to-face with the rise of Mussolini and Hitler, figures who deeply fascinated him. Appointed Minister of Labor following one such coup, Perón forged strong ties with unions and their leaders. He swiftly grasped the power of worker popularity, pioneering a brand of populism previously unseen among military or political figures.

It was during this transformative period that he met Eva Duarte, a young aspiring actress gaining fame through her radio shows and connections with the Argentine elite. Eva, born into poverty and out of wedlock, harbored deep resentment towards the wealthy. Excluded from her father's funeral by his legitimate family, she was determined to take from the rich and give to the poor, embodying the spirit of a modern social justice warrior. It was Eva who persuaded Perón to run for president, a campaign that led to his victory in the 1946 democratic elections.

Despite their initial rise through a military coup, Perón and Eva were ousted by a rival military faction. During Perón's imprisonment, Eva passionately defended him via radio broadcasts, rallying public support for his return. Bowing to this pressure, the military called for elections, which Perón won, marking the beginning of the 'Peronization of Argentina'—an era characterized by a unique form of homegrown fascism.

Railroads, phone companies, the Central Bank, utilities, etc. were all nationalized. Now they belonged to the people. If you had dissident thought you were most likely to be shut down, expropriated or incarcerated.

It is often narrated that upon Perón's ascension to power, the central bank aisles were 'not walkable' due to the abundance of gold bars stored there. However, by the end of his presidency, much of this gold had vanished and the central bank was empty.

1.4 EVITA LOVES ME, I LOVE EVITA

My father being a first grader during this time was taught in school that Juan Perón and Evita *loved him*. "Evita me Ama' 'Yo amo a Evita' (Evita loves me, I love Evita) was how he was taught to read and write *day after day* in school. School textbooks with colored drawings told children that Juan Perón fed the doves in the national square and that he was in a fight with the imperialists. Almost every single page deified General Perón and Evita as perfect beings, capable of caring for every child and family in Argentina. It was brainwashing from childhood for every Argentinean. They gave away toys, bicycles, food, houses and whatever it took to win votes. Today, Peronism uses the same methods, printing fiat money and giving it away in different ways. *Sound familiar in your country?*

The foreigner is bad and it is a good thing to 'combat capital'. Peronism has an anthem and they would force children to sing it every morning. It is even sung to this day because of it's catchy tunes by supporters and one of the main parts of the lyrics is 'Combating the capital'. They combated capital, and capital went where it was treated best...

Peronism (fascism-colectivism) was inculcated in schools and families. In my own family, my grandfather got into a knife fight with his brother over political issues, at a typical Sunday family lunch, and they didn't speak to each other for decades. This was 'normal' in those divided societies. Socialism has to divide to rule; it is their system. A direct road to ruin an entire country. Two provinces (states) of the country were named with the name of Eva Perón and Juan Perón, only because they was born there.

For more interesting historical content about Perón and Evita and the brainwashing since childhood, go to **arielaguilar.com/CONTENTBP**

1.5 A PERPETUAL MONETARY DISASTER

The resentment and envy against capitalists in Argentina has shaped its economic history, resulting in five different currencies and the removal of thirteen zeros from them. This transformation began in the 19th century, where Argentina experienced periods of monetary freedom. During this time, foreign coins competed with local coins, private banknotes, and provincial currencies. In 1881, Argentina unified its currencies under the first national currency, the Peso Moneda Nacional, which remained in circulation until 1969. Operating with a gold exchange standard for short periods, it marked the longest-running currency in Argentina's history. Notably,

Argentina lacked a central bank until 1935, coinciding with the introduction of a *temporary* income tax, which *remains in effect to this day...*

1.6 THIRTEEN ZEROS REMOVED FROM THE CURRENCY

Argentina has experienced cyclical economic collapses, each resulting in the devastating destruction of people's savings. Throughout its tumultuous history, the nation has faced recurring instances of monetary instability and economic upheaval. The first major instance of such instability occurred during the 19th century, a period when Argentina enjoyed monetary freedom but lacked the robust financial infrastructure needed to sustain it.

In the following sections, I will provide a concise yet comprehensive overview of the historical evolution of the currency in my homeland, tracing its journey from the early days of monetary freedom to the present challenges. This overview will highlight the key events and policies that have shaped Argentina's economic landscape and influenced the lives of its citizens.

Particular attention will be given to the hyperinflation episodes of the late 20th century, which severely impacted the nation's economy and eroded public trust in the financial system. The analysis will also cover the controversial currency board system implemented in the 1990s, which pegged the Argentine peso to the US dollar in an attempt to stabilize the economy, and its eventual collapse in the early 2000s.

Through this comprehensive examination, I aim to provide a deeper understanding of how Argentina's complex monetary history continues to shape the current economic conditions and the daily lives of its people. Next, we will delve into the evolution of the Argentine currency, exploring how each stage and transformation has influenced the country's economic and social context.

Peso Moneda Corriente 1826-1881

The peso *moneda corriente* was the currency of the province of Buenos Aires and initially had the same value as the 'peso fuerte', a gold-backed peso with an equivalence of 1 to 1. However, over time, the value of the currency was significantly devalued. By the end of its existence, the devaluation was so severe that it took 25 pesos 'Moneda Corriente' to obtain the same amount of gold that a single 'peso fuerte' could buy at the beginning. This drastic change highlights the economic instability and challenges the province faced in maintaining the value of its currency.

Note: These images depict specimen banknotes and have no monetary value. They are included in this book solely for illustrative and educational purposes.

Peso Moneda Nacional 1881 - 1969

The first unified national currency in Argentina was the 'Peso Moneda Nacional'. To obtain one unit of this new currency, you needed 25 units of the previous currency. Upon its launch, the 'Peso Moneda Nacional' was on par with the 'Peso Fuerte' (the gold peso) and enjoyed periods of gold convertibility until the establishment of the Central Bank in 1935. This currency served the nation until it was eventually replaced in 1970.

Peso Ley 18.188 1970-1983

To receive 1 'Peso Ley', 100 'Pesos Moneda Nacional' were needed. This currency eventually suffered such severe inflation that, by 1983, one million peso notes were in circulation. This hyperinflation significantly devalued the currency, reflecting the economic instability of the period.

Note: These images depict specimen banknotes and have no monetary value. They are included in this book solely for illustrative and educational purposes.

11

Peso Argentino 1983-1985

This was the shortest-lived currency in the region, completely destroyed in just two years. At the beginning of its brief existence, it took 10,000 'Pesos Ley' to obtain a single 'Peso Argentino'. With this new currency Argentina had already removed six zeros from the original Peso Moneda Nacional.

Note: These images depict specimen banknotes and have no monetary value. They are included in this book solely for illustrative and educational purposes..

12

Austral 1985-1992

The Austral Plan was an economic initiative introduced during Raúl Alfonsín's presidency to stabilize Argentina's economy and curb hyperinflation. As part of this plan, the Austral currency was introduced, replacing the Peso Argentino at an exchange rate of 10,000 to 1. Initially, the Austral was relatively strong, with 83 cents of an Austral equivalent to one US dollar. However, the currency's value quickly deteriorated. By the end of its seven-year lifespan, you needed ₳10,000 to buy the same dollar.

Note: These images depict specimen banknotes and have no monetary value. They are included in this book solely for illustrative and educational purposes.

Peso convertible 1992-2002

The Convertibility Law, enacted during the presidency of Carlos Menem with Domingo Cavallo as Minister of Economy, was remarkably concise. It stated that the new currency would come into circulation on the day the Austral reached an exchange rate of A10,000 to one dollar, and that this new peso would be convertible one to one with the US dollar. The peso's physical characteristics were modified to be identical to those of the dollar. To print one peso, the central bank needed to have one dollar in its reserves. This scheme resembled what many stablecoins, cryptocurrencies that seek to keep their price pegged to a certain asset, such as the US dollar, are trying to do today. Lasting almost ten years, this convertible peso provided Argentines with the only decade free of inflation, as prices remained virtually constant throughout the period.

Note: These images depict specimen banknotes and have no monetary value. They are included in this book solely for illustrative and educational purposes.

Peso 2002-today

After the late 2001 crisis, which I'll be discussing in a future section of the book, Argentina defaulted on the one-to-one promise, and the peso was no longer 'convertible'. The exchange rate soon went to 4 to 1, then below 3 to 1, and since then has been steadily climbing, now on its way to reaching 1000 pesos for one dollar as of this writing.

To sum up, if you had 250,000,000,000,000 pesos moneda corriente in 1870, you would have had to exchange the old currency for a new one, removing zeros, and you would end up with one peso of today. One peso, as of this writing, is worth less than 10% of a US cent.

Let's imagine for a moment that your father was the richest Argentinean in the country in 1969. Your father heeds the recommendation of Argentine politicians who say, 'save in national currency'. So your father proceeds to sell all his real estate, factories, land, art collection, stocks and bonds for the Argentine fiat currency of the day, the Peso Moneda Nacional. He would have done what the politicians had demanded of him: save in national currency and not be a 'vendepatria'.

Assuming he was the richest Argentinean in 1970 and he would have sold everything for $10,000,000,000,000,000 pesos 'Moneda Nacional', equivalent to 28 billion nominal dollars in 1970 since the exchange rate was 350 pesos moneda nacional to the dollar. Keep in mind that 28 billion 1970 dollars had a purchasing power equivalent to 2.8 trillion today's dollars (2.8 Trillion in English language, i.e. as if your father had a net worth equivalent to ten Elon Musks or Jeff Bezos put together).

Because your father trusted and followed the recommendations of successive Argentine governments, today you, as an heir, would have **less than one US cent.** Such is the destructive power of government fiat money.

These dramatic depreciations highlight the severe economic problems and hyperinflation that plagued Argentina for decades. Such is the destructive power of fiat money, and millions of Argentines have experienced it. It's a wealth destruction machine, a void, a black hole that sucks away your life energy.

Unfortunately this is not only happening in Argentina. All fiat currencies in the world are losing value, all are stealing from human labour. What varies between them is the speed at which they steal value.

Note: These banknotes are specimens and have no monetary value. They are included in this book for illustrative and educational purposes only.

Period	Currency	Amount in Argentine currency
1881-1970	Peso Moneda Nacional	10,000,000,000,000
1970-1983	Peso Ley	100,000,000,000
1983-1985	Peso Argentino	10,000,000
1985-1992	Austral	10,000
1992-2002	Peso convertible	1
2002-Today	Peso	1

1.7 MILITARY COUPS AND PERONISM - THE BEGINNING OF THE DECLINE

I return to this period in my country and to these characters because I consider that it was a crucial moment when things began to deteriorate.

In 1930, Argentina entered a period marked by coups d'état and military governments. As I mentioned earlier, in the 1940s, the nation witnessed the rise of Juan Domingo Perón, at the time an admirer of Mussolini and Hitler. Perón quickly rose to power, embracing the wave of European fascism, and became Argentina's most prominent populist leader, alongside his wife, Eva Duarte de Perón.

This constant change made it difficult for Argentina to have consistent and effective leadership, weakening political institutions and public confidence in the country.

Juan Domingo Perón came to power with a combination of populism and authoritarianism. By centralising power, he repressed opposition and limited democratic freedoms. This led to a government that did not encourage open political participation or dissent. Perón nationalised key industries such as the railways and the meatpacking industry, which meant that the government took control of these businesses. However, this often led to inefficiency and corruption. In addition, Perón's extensive social welfare programmes, while popular, put pressure on the national budget without increasing productivity.

During Perón's government, a system of widespread surveillance was established. Neighbourhood spies, known as 'manzaneras', watched residents, creating a climate of fear and stifling free speech. Perón and his wife Evita cultivated a majority of followers who were loyal and converted family members and descendants. Portraits of the couple were obligatory in public and private spaces, and Evita was revered as the 'spiritual leader of the nation'.

The authoritarian practices and economic policies established during Perón's rule influenced subsequent governments, creating a cycle of instability and ineffective governance. This legacy made it difficult for Argentina to recover and grow in a sustainable manner. These factors, combined, undermined Argentina's political stability and economic health, leading the country down a path of socialist decline that has had lasting effects. Understanding these reasons helps to explain the complex challenges facing Argentina today.

1.8 TENEMOS QUE VIVIR CON LO NUESTRO - WE HAVE TO LIVE WITH WHAT IS OURS

Argentina got into the culture that we had to develop the national industries and that meant 'buying Argentine' and not foreign products. This policy of 'product substitution' has been tried for the last 80 years without success and is repeated again and again in the media, in the clasrooms. However, the country is not a leading example of industrial production. This led to the closure of imports, to the nationalization of railroads, phone companies, power utilities, airlines, etc.

We had the same cars being manufactured from the 60s till the beginning of the 90s. Only a handful of models were offered, with insignificant upgrades through the decades. If you requested to have a phone line installed in your home, you had to wait between **10 to 20 years** for the state run phone company to install it. This meant that a house that had a phone could cost twice the price of a house without a phone. Just like the Soviet Union.

1.9 ARGENTINA'S INFATUATION WITH THE US DOLLAR

Argentines currently hold more than 200 billion dollars in cash, where one in ten physical banknotes that have been printed is in Argentina. According to these estimates, two out of every ten banknotes outside the US are in the country. We have also learned the hard way that dollars should not be kept in a bank account, as these are usually confiscated every decade or two. Therefore, Argentines save in cash either at home or in private or bank safety deposit boxes. Houses and cars are bought in cash, literally by bringing 300,000 US dollars to the signature table and counting every note. The mortgage lending market is virtually non-existent because a payment system cannot be planned in an environment of volatile inflation.

In 2023, the average salary in Argentina was 300 dollars per month and the square metre of a house ranges from 1,000 to 2,000 dollars, depending on the area (equivalent to 90 to 180 dollars per square foot). In order to buy a square metre, an Argentinean who saves 50 dollars a month (almost 17 per cent of his salary) could buy a single square metre every 30 months. People must either save illegally in foreign currency (as the purchase of dollars is prohibited) or invest in something and then pay for their house in cash.

1.10 PRESIDENT RAUL ALFONSÍN

His election symbolized the return to democracy and hope for a brighter future. However, Alfonsín faced immense challenges, particularly hyper-inflation, which spiraled out of control during his presidency due to the persistent, *never-ending-story,* enduring belief in government intervention at all levels.

During Raúl Alfonsín's government hyperinflation skyrocketed to astronomical levels, with *monthly inflation peaks surpassing 200%* in some cases. At its most critical moment, annual inflation reached ***levels close to 5,000%*** in 1989.

For Argentines, enduring such a monstrous annual inflation rate profoundly affected daily life in a number of ways. Consider this scenario: you buy a loaf of bread in the morning for 1 unit of currency, only to find that its price triples or quadruples by the afternoon. And in as little as a week, that same loaf could skyrocket to 50 units. In a month, it could reach a staggering 500 units, making basic necessities unaffordable for many. This rapid inflation severely erodes purchasing power, leading to widespread uncertainty, instability and hardship for individuals and businesses.

In the midst of this hyperinflation, the amount of physical banknotes needed for simple everyday purchases at the supermarket increased exponentially. What once could be bought with a handful of bills now demanded stacks upon stacks of cash! Imagine needing a thick, brick-like wad of bills just to cover the cost of groceries for a single shopping trip... Those who wanted to buy a car or a house moved around with briefcases full of banknotes or disguised them in plastic bags. This overabundance of paper currency became a visual representation of the economic chaos, as individuals struggled to manage and transport the sheer volume of money needed for even the most basic transactions.

Alfonsín left his presidency in advance, due to the failures of the socialist and Keynesian economic policies that he implemented. Facing immense pressure and a loss of public confidence, he resigned in 1989, calling for elections before schedule. This power vacuum was filled by Peronist Carlos Menem, who assumed the presidency early and inherited the monumental task of stabilising the Argentine economy.

1.11 THE 90s - LA FIESTA MENEMISTA

We call it the Menemist Party, not because it was a political party, but because the 90s felt like an economic boom for part of the population, felt *like a party* at least for some. For the first time in decades, Argentina had monetary stability, no inflation, real economic growth at meaningful rates, and money and products were flowing in. If you had your own small business, it was easy to make thousands of dollars per month. Home mortgages became available again after decades (imagine a country with no home mortgages), and all the deficit-ridden, failing state companies were privatized (phone lines, trains, power generation, airlines). Imports of foreign products were allowed, and we started having modern cars after decades of manufacturing the same models since the mid-1960s. Now, you could get a phone line in days instead of decades. Prices almost did not change for a decade. Menem removed compulsory military service after a soldier died of exhaustion. For an Argentine, it was more affordable to go to Miami, New York, or Europe; we were once again recognized as tourists who spent a lot of money overseas. Prices in the US were actually cheaper than in Argentina. Because of this, it was as convenient for Argentines to spend their holidays in Orlando and Miami as it was to go to the trend-setting beach towns of Argentina and Uruguay, which were more expensive.

1.12   THE DOWNSIDE TO THE 90S

During the previous inflationary decades, it was almost futile for the government to collect much in taxes. As soon as the money was in the hands of the government, it was devalued due to inflation, so Argentina did not put much effort into tax collection.

When Menem with his economy minister Domingo Cavallo, instituted the tether to the dollar, at the one-to-one peg of the convertibility, he soon had to resort to other forms of government financing. This included raising taxes, creating new ones, and setting up high import tariffs to protect the 'national industry'. He re-entered Argentina into the international bond markets, but continuously accumulated more debt in dollars. The privatization of state companies resulted in the creation of private monopolies. For example, you could only choose one phone company depending on where you lived.

In 1995, Mexico entered into a recession that had a ripple effect on other Latin American countries. This event became known as the 'Tequila Effect'.

As a free market advocate, my father went on television to explain why Argentina still needed to lower its taxes to ensure a path to greatness. At the time, Argentina had raised VAT from 18 to 21%, we had 35% income tax, a 35% import duty on many foreign products, and a 33% social tax on labor, along with over a hundred other taxes.

1.13   THE LABOUR LAWS

Additionally, Argentina still has archaic labor laws that make it extremely difficult, burdensome and risky to fire an employee; employers have to pay one month's severance for each year of employment plus 33% of salary goes to social security. As an interesting fact, much more recently, during the pandemic, this penalty was doubled, which meant that if an employer had to fire an employee who had been working in his company for 10 years, he would have to pay him 20 months' salary as a penalty.

Not only that but there is an *industry of labour judicial processes*. Since complying with the laws and regulations is so onerous, many employers and employees work 'in the black'. Non registered jobs to save on taxes and procedures. However the law included severe penalties for whoever does this. The outcome of this is that this suing employers industry erupted and it is so pervasive and profitable that even that someone who has never, ever worked for you can claim in the justice system that he was your employee and you payed him 'in the black', 'under the table'. Since labour trials take more than five years to settle in court your lawyer will most likely advice you to just 'settle this out of court' and pay something.

1.14   THE 'MONOTRIBUTO'

A positive child of the 90's is the Argentine 'monotributo', a simplified tax regime designed for small businesses, freelancers, and self-employed individuals. This people pay a fixed amount according to revenue brackets. Under this regime, your businesse is exempt from filing for VAT and Income Taxes and you don't have to pay them! You just pay 'one tribute'. The lowest tier of revenue ranged from 1,000 to 12,000 USD per month back when it was introduced in 1998. In exchange, businesses only had to pay around 5% of their revenue to the government and could do self-reporting without the need for an accountant. The value of the dollar was much higher when the monotributo was launched in 1998 than it is today, so after adjusting for inflation, those 12,000 USD are now equivalent to over 20,000 USD per month today. Imagine being able to generate revenues of 240,000 USD per year, and only having to file a single self-made report and pay 5% of that, saving you from having to pay the 21% VAT tax and 35% Income Tax. Once businesses were set up in the monotributo, they didn't want to surpass the monthly limit and risk being changed by our tax revenue service to the 'General Regime,' which required paying VAT and Income tax.

Where does the *monotributo* stand now?

At the beginning of 2024, the lowest bracket allowed income of up to 2.1 million pesos per year (approximately 142 USD per month at the current rate), with the highest level allowing income of up to 17 million pesos (1,150 USD per month). This is a far cry from the USD 12,000 per month that could be declared in the late 1990s. Fortunately, with the latest update under the administration of Javier Milei, the monotributo system in Argentina has undergone significant changes. The lowest bracket now allows annual income of up to 6.5 million pesos (approximately USD 400 monthly turnover at the current rate), while the highest bracket allows income of up to 68 million pesos (approximately USD 4,200 per month). This represents a substantial improvement on previous figures, making it a very advantageous system for the self-employed.

1.15 PRESIDENT DE LA RUA

After Menem, Argentina got its very own Joe Biden in the form of Fernando de la Rúa in late 1999. This elderly man rose to power from a left-leaning political coalition and became famous for his sluggishness, slurred speech, and tendency to get lost on stage. He would often claim, "*They say I am boring...*" During his campaign, he promised to lower taxes and claimed he knew how to do it. However, his first measure in office, introduced on the very first day, was to implement new taxes and raise some of the existing ones. For instance, he introduced income taxes for employees (who were already paying 33% in social security taxes; now it was 33% plus up to 35% in income tax) and raised and introduced other taxes. The economy took a nosedive, putting a significant brake on an economy that was already in recession. His vice president resigned, and the coalition that brought him to power started to crack. Unemployment rose to double digits.

1.16 COUNTRY RISK

When I was a teenager, I remember turning on the news every morning as the country plunged into a recession, which I would consider a depression. The unemployment rate climbed to approximately 18.3%, the economy was stagnant, and conditions worsened daily. Each morning, the news would report not only the day's weather but also Argentina's steadily rising country risk:

450... 489... 513... 590... 643...

What was this number, and why would we check on it every day as it loomed on us, the end of times? Country risk is the difference between the interest rate a country pays on its debt and the interest rate that the US government pays on its debt. US Treasuries are considered 'risk-free' (that's what they say; you are actually losing purchasing power 99% of the time). Country risk is measured in 'basis points,' a method of expressing percentages as integer numbers, with one basis point equaling 0.01%. Thus, an interest rate of 4.5% translates to 450 basis points. If Argentina had a country risk of 590 basis points and the U.S. had a T-Bill interest rate of 2.5%, it meant Argentina was paying 8.4% on its debt.

1.17 THE IMF'S ROLE

TV news shows would tell how the government was dependent on the meetings and agreements with the International Monetary Fund. The IMF would loan money to Argentina, demand changes in its economic policy, and since the Argentine bonds were sliding, the country risk was on the rise. Eventually, Argentina was not going to be able to repay not just the capital on its loans but the interest on them as well. The default was looming.

The IMF demanded austerity measures and more taxes. These policies were badly received by the public in general and so attempts were made to cut spending, soon to be taken back. The general sentiment was that the IMF was going to put down the finger on Argentina.

1.18 THE 2001 CORRALITO - THE 'LITTLE CORRAL'

Corralito means 'little or tiny corral', a pen for livestock, as in the corral where you put animals on a farm. That is what this economic measure of the government was called. We woke up on December 1st, 2001, to the news that withdrawals from bank accounts were severely limited, capped at around 250 USD per week. All the rest of your pesos and dollars became trapped inside the banking system, where you could only pay with debit and credit cards, checks, or wire transfers. The minister of economy thought that since most economic transactions would pass through a bank, then tax revenues would go up. Sound familiar?

International wire transfers were also halted. Only a few thousand people managed to get their money out, as some resorted to the justice system and initiated an expedited judicial procedure known as 'Appeal for protection', in which a judge had to rule within 48 hours. There were some well-known judges who consistently ruled in favor of the savers. Once the judge granted a court order, it was given to you. Then, you had to find a policeman on the street and request his accompaniment to the bank to have the order enforced. Banks complied and paid only those savers who presented court orders.

1.19 'CORRALÓN', LOOTING, RIOTS AND THE CRYING CHINESE

Then, the looting of supermarkets, trucks, and small shops began. Rumors swirled that the opposition leader had struck a deal with the provincial police to organize and allow the looting to occur without repercussions.

Some people became known as 'piqueteros' or picketers, protesting by blockading streets and bridges, burning tires, and disrupting the free flow of traffic and people. Some of them even demanded tolls to allow passage. Other citizens of good will helped by organizing popular pots, in which stews were given for free or at very low prices.

Since the 90s, many mini-markets have been operated by immigrants from East Asia. During the December looting, viewers across several TV channels witnessed the live ransacking of a shop owned by an oriental businessman, Wang Zhao. As his life's work was destroyed before his eyes, he was overcome with despair, releasing a heart-wrenching cry that resonated through the airwaves, capturing the nation's attention.

As many others, this shop owner lost everything on that fateful day, but has since gradually regained his footing over the years. Argentina often provides new opportunities…

1.20 ARBOLITOS Y CUEVAS - LITTLE TREES AND CAVES

At the close of 2001, amidst the country's economic collapse, the implementation of the Corralito and the persistence of the convertibility law were yet realities. Despite day's news, depicting a stable exchange rate, whereby one peso purportedly equaled one dollar, I remember that a man, cloaked in a heavy coat, paid a visit to my father's business store. He would offer him 1.15 pesos for every dollar provided. Since my father used to sell most of his products for dollars, witnessing him make a 15% instant extra money amazed me! What was going on? Who was this man in the beige coat? My father replied: He is an *arbolito* (little tree). *Arbolitos* are men that hang out in the downtown streets of Buenos Aires shouting: *Cambio! Cambio!* (Exchange! Exchange!). You approach them, ask them their price, strike a deal and he will walk you to the "*cueva*", he will take you to the cave. Don't be scared, the 'cave' there is just a point where black market or free market, currency exchange operations take place, dealing mainly with exchanging pesos to dollars and dollars to pesos in Argentina.. I've seen *cuevas* that are clothing stores, antique shops, numismatic shops, hotels, offices of the stock brokerage houses inside of the Buenos Aires Stock Exchange, the local shop that copies your keys and by far the most common ones are the travel agent agencies.

Anybody can become or be running a *cueva* in Argentina. If all the *cuevas* could be shut down tomorrow morning the country would collapse by the next day. Imagine having to go to a bank where you will get less than half the pesos if you sell your dollars. The bank and government will let you sell unlimited amounts of dollars at the government official rate. Yet in order to maintain an artificial low price they will only allow you to buy back only 200 dollars per month!, and coupled with an additional tax burden, typically amounting to 30%, plus an additional 35% surcharge. The free market operation of the Cuevas are what allow the country to continue functioning. Be sure to thank your '*cuevero', man of the cave* when you meet him. The little corral soon led to the 'large corral' or *corralón*. It meant that you couldn't even withdraw the $250 per week that was previously allowed.

1.21 THE CURFEW AND THE CACEROLAZO

On Thursday December 19th, 2001 president De La Rua appeared on national television and announced a nationwide curfew. You were not allowed to leave your home between 8pm and 6am.

The broadcast ended with the thunderous sound of pots and pans being banged, used as instruments of protest in almost every citizen's homes.

It was called a *cacerolazo* or 'big pot protest'. The announcement of the curfew only fuelled more riots and protests the next day, spreading throughout the country, but particularly intensifying in the most famous square, Plaza de Mayo. The government responded by deploying police and military forces to suppress the attacks of the protesters, even resorting to sending out police on horses to retaliate. Tragically, over 20 people lost their lives that day in the protests.

1.22 THE HELICOPTER ESCAPE

On December 20th, we all watched it live on TV: the presidential helicopter landed atop the roof of the Pink House (Argentina's White House). President De La Rua announced his resignation, boarded the helicopter, and fled from the executive government building's roof. With the vice-president having resigned months before, the country was left without a president.

For more interesting historical content about the Corralito, the curfew and this period in Argentina, go to : **arielaguilar.com/CONTENTBP**

1.23 FIVE DIFFERENT PRESIDENTS IN TWO WEEKS AND CONGRESS CELEBRATING THE DEFAULT

De la Rúa's resignation created a power vacuum, leading to a rapid turnover of five interim presidents in Argentina over two weeks, reflecting a severe political and economic crisis:

Fernando de la Rúa (1999-2001): Resigned amid economic turmoil and protests on December 20, 2001.

Ramón Puerta: Senate President, briefly held the presidency for a few hours on December 21, 2001.

Adolfo Rodríguez Saá: Took office but resigned after one week on December 30, 2001, after declaring Argentina's debt default.

Eduardo Camaño: Served as interim president from December 30 to 31, 2001.

Eduardo Duhalde: Became president on January 2, 2002, and led until May 2003, implementing a devaluation and 'asymmetric pesification'. He also paved the way for Néstor Kirchner's presidency.

I still recall the rare experience of returning to the forgotten inflation, purchasing a cheeseburger from McDonald's, which had been priced at 99 cents for a decade, only to find that it now was priced at 1.99 pesos...! Yes, overnight, the price of my go-to hamburger had doubled.

Later, in a few days, the decoupling of the peso from the dollar caused the exchange rate to go from *1 to 1* to *4 to 1*. If you had saved pesos, suddenly you had only 25% of your original sum. Houses and cars, when measured in dollars, were at their lowest prices in history, presenting a *tremendous opportunity* for those who had saved dollars in cash at home.

1.24 WHOEVER DEPOSITED DOLLARS WILL GET DOLLARS, WHOEVER DEPOSITED PESOS WILL GET PESOS- THE END OF CONVERTIBILITY LAW

Difficult days for my beloved country. In short, due to the application of the 'Ley de Acefalía', *Acephaly Law,* four interim presidents were elected in a few days, and finally Eduardo Duhalde was elected fifth. He had won 30% of the vote in the 1999 elections and was rumoured to have organised the looting to destabilise the De la Rúa government. In his inaugural speech, he said his now famous phrase: *'Whoever deposited dollars will receive dollars, whoever deposited pesos will receive pesos'*, to reassure Congress and the public, and received a standing ovation. A few weeks later, we had the asymmetrical pesification, where the only thing we got were.... pesos.

I still remember the rare experience of facing inflation again, buying a McDonald's cheeseburger, which had been 99 cents for a decade, only to discover that it now cost 1.99 pesos.... Yes, overnight, the price of my favourite burger had doubled! And so had the price of so many other things....

Later, in a few days, the decoupling of the peso from the dollar caused the exchange rate to go from *1 to 1* to *4 to 1*. If you had saved in pesos, suddenly you could only buy 25% of the dollars you would have been able to buy a few days earlier. Houses and cars, measured in dollars, were at their lowest prices in decades, presenting an *incredible opportunity* for those who had saved dollars in cash at home.

1.25 THE ASYMMETRIC PESIFICATION

The Duhalde law stated that whoever deposited dollars or had debts denominated in dollars, now had or owed 1.40 pesos for every dollar. This meant that if you had saved 10,000 USD in the bank, your dollar account balance was now 0, and your peso account balance increased by 14,000 pesos. Meanwhile, the free market exchange rate for pesos to dollars was now *4 to 1*. So, if you wanted to take those 14,000 pesos and buy back dollars at the *4 to 1* exchange rate, you would only get 3,500 USD. In other words, you lost 65% of what you had saved. The opposite was true if you had debts or a mortgage denominated in dollars. If you owed 100,000 USD for your house, now you owed 140,000 pesos, which at the *4 to 1* exchange rate meant you now just owed 35,000 USD. Savers were wiped out, and debtors were pardoned – typical fiat money behavior.

Given the history of devaluations and deposit confiscations in the past, Argentina teaches you ***not to trust banks and institutions***. Banks and institutions are not safe, you have to save yourself. As a consequence, we have cultivated a culture of saving dollars in physical banknotes, ***in cash***.

1.26 THE RETURN OF INFLATION - THE NON LEGISLATED TAX

Since the day President Eduardo Duhalde took us out of the convertibility law, we have returned to inflation. — an inflation that steadily rose, little by little. Initially, the rate stood at merely 10%, although the method of calculation remains obscure to me. This ambiguity persists, especially considering that I observed prices doubling shortly after the abandonment of convertibility. Most likely, they simply began counting from percentages that suited their convenience: 10%, 15%, 20%, 30%, 50%... This situation escalated to a point of insanity, with Argentina experiencing inflation rates surpassing 100% annually. This means that your peso savings *lose more than half of their value every year*!

The Argentine constitution states that every tax must be legislated by the national congress; however, *the amount of money the country can print is not specified*. The ultimate objective remains consistent: to finance the expenditures of the various branches of government. Instead of collecting taxes and enacting laws, why not simply print the necessary money without undergoing the legislative process? The outcome remains unchanged: **increasing the money supply devalues the purchasing power of individuals holding pesos, as well as dollars, euros, yen and other fiat currencies**. Effectively eroding, *stealing* their wealth through inflation, often without them even realizing what is happening. So not only does Argentina have over 50% taxation pressure but the fact that there is now in 2023, over 100% inflation per year means that your savings are *taxed at over 50% per year*.

I make a simple logical reasoning: If your government taxes you on 50% of everything you earn, and then taxes you with another 50% on everything that buy, and then takes half of your savings every year through a 100% inflation rate per year, meaning your savings go to half in purchasing power each successive year, *are you really free?*

1.27 'EL INDEC MIENTE' - THE CPI LIES

After the 2001 default Argentina no longer had access to international credit markets. So in order to continue issuing bonds it created inflation-adjusted peso bonds, offering investors an interest rate plus the inflation rate. Consequently, after this bond issue the government began to falsify inflation data in order to pay less interest. For example, during Cristina Kirchner's initial presidency (we will analyse her presidency later), the government claimed that inflation was only 10% per year when in reality it was close to 30%. This manipulation allowed Argentina to withhold, i.e. *steal*, billions in interest payments from bondholders.

The INDEC, the government agency in charge of statistics, became notorious during those years with the popular phrase 'El INDEC miente' (The INDEC lies). And it is not only the Argentine government; most governments manipulate and lie about inflation numbers. While the US and Europe cite around 10% annual inflation, my travels with *La Bitcoineta** have *unveiled a starkly different reality*. When I asked people in Europe about their experience of inflation from 2020 till now, most answers ranged between *30%, 50%*, and even *100%*.

*Bitcoineta is an initiative aimed at promoting Bitcoin adoption and education, particularly in areas where access to financial services may be limited. It involves traveling in a van, to various communities in LatAm & Europe to provide information, resources, and support related to Bitcoin.

1.28 THE 'VULTURE FUNDS' OR JUST PLAIN OLD SOVEREIGN HEDGE FUNDS

Let us now consider, by way of introduction to the subject, the hedge funds: they are private companies that raise capital from investors and employ a management team to seek opportunities to grow that capital. The typical business model for hedge funds is as follows:

Capital is raised, typically around 100 million USD, from various sources, including wealthy families, individual investors, corporations, pension funds, and other entities seeking high yields or returns on investment. The hedge fund manager typically offers the following arrangement to these investors: "*For managing your money, I will charge a 2% fee per year.*" So, right from the start, the hedge fund has an annual budget of 2 million USD. However, if the hedge fund generates a profit *with your money*, they retain 20% of that profit and distribute the remaining 80% to the investors.

For instance, if the hedge fund achieves a 15% return on investment on a 100 million fund, it yields a total profit of 15 million USD. Consequently, the hedge fund can claim 20% of that profit, which amounts to 3 million USD, in addition to the 2 million management fee, resulting in a total income of 5 million USD for managing other people's money.

At times, managers make incorrect decisions, resulting in financial losses rather than gains. For instance, the fund could be down 15%, translating to a loss of 15 million in a year. In such a scenario, the hedge fund is only entitled to the 2 million management fee. While some hedge funds opt to take the 2 million fee, others choose to waive it, refraining from charging their investors for the losses incurred.

I recommend the book 'More Money Than God', (*Sebastian Mallaby, Penguin Press 2010*) to learn about the history of ten different hedge funds and how these managers have to make daily bets that can result in a 500 million profit or loss in a day! Imagine having the nerves to make such a decision.

Now, to the story of Argentina, and its relationship with *sovereign hedge funds* or how politicians and the media of Argentina like to call it: *The Vulture Funds*. Vulture, as in the bird that feeds off the deceased animals. These funds have a contrarian view about the economic decisions of populist governments, betting against them. While governments, the media, the academia and most of the people think that decision A is the correct decision and here come these hedge funds with the opposite view of reality and economics and say, no, the correct path is the opposite, decision B. These fund managers believe that decision A is incorrect, flawed and will eventually cause more harm than good. And so they find a way to bet against A and go for B.

They end up being right most of the times and making billions of dollars in the process.

Paul Singer, a hedge fund manager, decided to buy Argentine bonds at pennies on the dollar during the 2002 default on Argentina's debt. Because Argentina had defaulted on its obligations and was not paying its debtors, bonds that were once worth 100 cents could be purchased on the market for around 18 cents on the dollar.

He realized, as many other investors did, that if Argentina ever wanted to return to being a part of the global economy, it would have to emerge from its state of bankruptcy or default. Argentina adopted a short-term view, while these investors adopted a long-term view, willing to wait years or decades until Argentina started repaying. Additionally, they had the patience and the financial resources to take legal action. Countries continuously issue bonds to raise money for the government. When the original bonds were issued, Argentina had agreed to be subject to New York law, as issuing the bonds under Argentine legislation and courts would not have attracted as much capital.

Paul Singer and others took this to court for years and eventually settled with the country for billions in profit.

For years, Argentines heard from President Cristina Kirchner, the incessant media, and universities that these are 'vulture funds' and that it's not okay for them to demand what's in the contract. They argue that these funds do not have a social view of the world and that debtors should not claim what is rightfully theirs if they are making so much money off of it.

What Cristina and the media are not telling is that if it wasn't for the existence of these hedge funds buying billions of dollars of Argentine bonds at 20 cents on the dollar, those bonds *would have gone even lower!* If nobody is buying and there are only sellers, prices plummet to zero. Is all the bluff perhaps because these politicians even wanted the bonds to go even lower for them to buy them perhaps at 10 cents? 5 cents? 1 cent? Then get to power and repay the debtors and scoop a 20 to 100 times return?

1.29 NESTOR KIRCHNER - THE PRESIDENT THAT WON WITH 22% OF THE VOTES AND COULDN'T ACCOUNT FOR THE WHEREABOUTS OF 500 MILLION DOLLARS OF HIS PROVINCE

He was known as the *Penguin of Santa Cruz*, referring to his association with one of Argentina's southernmost provinces. He had been ruling as governor and had turned their province into a little fiefdom of state workers. Rumors circulated that he had taken 500 million dollars from the province coffers and invested it offshore, never to be seen again. After one and a half years in power, President Duhalde decided to call for elections and supported the *Penguin*, Nestor Kirchner. Nestor ran and received 22% of the votes, while the main candidate, Carlos Menem, the former president from 1989 to 1999, received 25% of the votes.

According to Argentine rules, when a candidate receives a low percentage of votes and there is a small difference between the first and second place candidates, a 'Ballotage' is triggered, which means the election is held again with only the first and second place candidates. Sadly for Argentina's history, the third place candidate, Ricardo Lopez Murphy, a classical liberal, received only 19% of the votes, so he was left outside the runoff. Because of Duhalde's support, this almost unknown Nestor Kirchner managed to get in second place. The polls indicated that if the election were held, Menem was going to lose, so he decided to forego his chance, cancel the Ballotage and Nestor Kirchner became proclaimed president of Argentina.

One of the darkest moments in Argentine history, he changed the course of the country, steering it away from the direction it had taken in the 90s and adopting a model similar to that of the 60s, 70s, and 80s. Inflation returned, export taxes were reinstated, and the mantra of '*let's defend national industries*' resurfaced.

1.30 CEPO CAMBIARIO - THE EXCHANGE CLAMP

When Nestor Kirchner's reelection moment arrived, he proposed his wife, Cristina Fernandez de Kirchner, to run for president. Many speculated that their strategy was to alternate the presidency between them, circumventing the two-term limit for each president. This way, they could effectively run as a family for as long as they continued to win the popular vote. However, these plans were abruptly halted when Nestor suddenly died under mysterious circumstances. There was never an autopsy conducted, and his body was only seen in a closed casket. Conspiracy theories suggest that it was his own family who had him killed.

Shortly after Nestor's death, Cristina decided to set one of her classic *interventionists* policies in 2011, 'El cepo cambiario'. *Cepo* in Spanish is the same word you use for *clamp* or *caliper*, that which is used on a car wheel to prevent its movement when you forgot to pay your parking permit.

That's what Argentines got: *a clamp on every Argentine's leg.*

This exchange lock meant that you could no longer freely trade pesos for dollars. You could sell all the dollars you wanted, but if you wanted to buy them back again, you had to log in to the tax authority website. There, you would input the amount you intended to purchase, and the website would give you an answer: either a 'yes' or a 'no.' If granted a 'yes,' you would then be able to go to your bank to exchange pesos for dollars. Otherwise, you would have to keep waiting or try another lower amount. *Kirchneristas* claimed that a computer assessment determined whether individuals could purchase dollars based on their incomes, properties, and other factors. However, since the algorithm remained undisclosed, officials could use their discretion, granting dollar buying abilities to their allies while refusing others at will.

The Kirchnerism governed in Argentina for three, (in real four) presidential terms: Néstor Kirchner assumed the presidency in 2003 and was succeeded by his wife, Cristina Fernández de Kirchner, who held the office from 2007 until 2015. From 2019 until 2023 Alberto Fernandez, a 'puppet' of Cristina Fernandez, became president while Cristina served as vice-president .

This political movement, derived from the most leftist Peronism, was characterized by its socialist-demagogic and irrational collectivist ideas. Many of their members were young terrorists during the 70s.

1.31 'EL DOLAR BLUE'

As a result of the *cepo*, the *blue* dollar, the informal 'black market' dollar, gained prominence. In fact, it represents the true value of the dollar, determined by market supply and demand.

While the official exchange rate was 4 pesos to a dollar, the real free market dollar rose to 6 pesos to a dollar, offering a 50% premium for those selling dollars for pesos. This gap persisted until 2015 when the official exchange rate reached 10 pesos to a dollar, and the dollar blue climbed to 15 pesos.

1.32 THE CAT AND MOUSE CHASE / THE RULO

When you exchange your dollar bills for peso bills at a *cueva* and receive 50% extra money, it means you could buy cheap dollars, sell them for more pesos, buy the cheap dollars again, and repeat the process. In Argentina, we refer to this as 'doing the rulo,' which is similar to saying 'doing the barrel roll,' 'doing the loop,' or 'doing the curly. We sometimes call it doing the financial bicycle. Almost everybody tries to get this free money, but the government started to put restrictions on who can receive dollars, and the amount of dollars allowed, to put an end to the *rulo*.

During the initial months, Argentines would travel to the neighboring country of Uruguay, specifically to the closest city of Colonia del Sacramento, to visit the casinos with their credit cards. They would use their peso-denominated credit cards to purchase casino chips, promptly exchange those chips for US dollar bills, return to Argentina with the physical cash, exchange the bills for more peso bills at any *cueva*, pay off the credit card, and repeat the process endlessly. Free money...

Despite the government's ongoing imposition of controls, taxes, and limits, Argentines continue to find ways to circumvent these restrictions and regulations. The reward is too high if you manage to accomplish it, at the beginning of the writing of this book in 2023, the spread between the official government rate and what the market is paying for the dollar sat at over 100% difference. This means that whoever has access to official dollars can effectively double their money if they spend them in the black market. It's not an easy feat, but consider the opportunities for corruption that this presents. If the government authorizes you to import a good, you'll pay for it in pesos at the official rate. However, if the dollar is freed a few months later, whatever you bought is now worth double the money. This system also enables discretionary permits, where friends of the government are granted the privilege to import goods at half price. All of this is financed by the impoverishment of the population through the inflation tax.

1.33 PRESIDENT MACRI

Mauricio Macri office as president from 2015 to 2019. He came from a rich family of a known magnate of industry, Franco Macri. He worked with his family but decided to venture out in the 90s by running in the elections of the most important soccer team in the country, Boca Juniors, which he won, turning the club around and making it win many tournaments. Then he decided to venture into politics by becoming mayor of the city of Buenos Aires for two terms and then running for president against Cristina Fernandez's candidate, Daniel Scioli. Macri won in 2015, bringing an end to twelve years of Kirchnerismo.

One of his first policies was to end the 'exchange clamp' and open up the economy. The official dollar Cristina left, was at 10 pesos to a dollar, while the blue dollar was at 15 pesos to a dollar. Once Macri freed the dollar, it quickly rose to 15, then slowly lowered to about 13 pesos to a dollar. He ran his presidential campaign with a 'zero inflation' and 'zero poverty' motto, but even though his economists were estimating only 10% inflation, he only managed to increase inflation during his mandate.

It also began adjusting the prices of services such as electricity and natural gas, which were subsidised by the state and had been kept ridiculously low in dollar terms due to years of frozen prices.

1.34 HOW TO STEAL A BILLION DOLLARS

Macri introduced a very particular monetary policy. Peso money was printed at scale to finance the deficit. In order to prevent all these new pesos being used to purchase of dollars and the exchange rate climbing with inflation they decided to offer short-term government bonds that payed over or around the inflation rate. So where is the stealing part? In that they were artificially suppressing the price of the dollar on the other end by selling central bank reserves. The exchange became locked at 20 pesos to a dollar when the government bonds were paying 30% annual yield. That meant that as long as the government didn't devalue the exchange rate you were making a 30% yield in dollar terms.

Macri managed to get Argentina's largest loan in history, 100 billion dollars from the IMF. It was announced as a great resource to build public infrastructure, yet it was mostly used by the central bank to keep the peso exchange rate suppressed. Once we ran out of those 100 billion the exchange rate rose to 40 pesos to a dollar.

Imagine for a second having the information on what you're going to do with the 100 billion. You could call your friend, partner, or trustee and say, 'Leverage up, baby! We're going to hold onto these peso bonds with a 30-40% annual yield for a few more months! I'll let you know when we're running out of the IMF loan and stop suppressing the peso price, and you can dump the bonds for dollars the week before. All legal, baby, no one will ever know! Leverage up, take a 10X position, '*Tenemos la vaca atada*,' an Argentine expression meaning '*The cow is tied up.*' We're going to win with 100% certainty, we're going to make billions at the expense of the Argentine population.

I cannot personally prove that Macri or any other politician for that matter or allies, with the same keynesian economic policies 'has stolen the money'. All I say is that it's easy to pull through without anybody being able to prove if it was done or not. Keynesianism is a perfect tool for stealing.

1.35 THE RETURN OF THE KIRCHNERISTAS

Cristina Kirchner wanted to return to power, but knew that she would not win directly, so she choose a *puppet* to run as her president, with herself as vice-president. Argentina has mandatory primary elections where the whole country has to vote on who the candidates for the general election is going to be. Alberto Fernandez, 'the puppet', ran with a clear advantage over Macri. This was an advance of what was going to come in the general elections so that Sunday night, the 40 pesos to dollar exchange rate quickly rose to 60 on Monday morning, to reflect what was coming.

Alberto Fernandez won and returned Argentina to the classic statist Kirchnerist model, exchange clamps, blue dollar, authorizations to import foreign products, etc. Not only that, but AF implemented one of the longest closures of any country during the COVID pandemic, lasting from March through approximately October or November 2020. It continued with varying levels of intensity and restrictions throughout 2021. The level of irrationality and authoritarianism was off the charts.

1.36 THE 'SOLIDARITY TAX'

The "solidarity tax" (PAIS) in Argentina, introduced in December 2019 under President Alberto Fernández, applies a 30% surcharge on purchases made in foreign currencies. This includes international travel, foreign services, and foreign currency purchases for savings.

The tax aims to generate revenue for social programs and curb the outflow of foreign currency reserves. For individuals, the solidarity tax makes foreign goods and services more expensive. This can affect those who travel abroad, buy products from international retailers, or subscribe to services like streaming platforms billed in foreign currency. The tax was part of yet another attempt to address the fiscal deficit without reducing public spending, placing the burden on the middle class.

1.37 HOW INFLATION STEALS FROM YOU IN INCOME TAX

As the fiat currency is depreciated, the purchasing power is reduced, making the fiat currency holder poorer and poorer... And not only that, inflation can erode your income through the phenomenon known as "bracket creep" in income taxation. As inflation increases, nominal wages may rise to keep pace with higher living costs.

However, if tax brackets and deductions aren't adjusted for inflation, taxpayers can find themselves pushed into higher tax brackets, resulting in a larger portion of their income being taxed at higher rates.

This effectively increases their tax burden, even though their real purchasing power hasn't improved. Thus, inflation can lead to higher income taxes without an actual increase in real income, diminishing overall financial well-being. This is an everyday issue in Argentine life.

The same issue happens with Capital Gains Tax, you are paying because your assets appreciated due to inflation, not because they went up in real value. You are being taxed for being stolen through the inflationary tax.

1.38 HOW DO YOU PUT UP WITH THIS?

When I tell the history of Argentina to people of Europe or other first world countries I often get asked: *How do you people put up with this sh*t??* The answer is that most Argentines usually repeat, without logic or deeper research, that this is the way to grow. But the facts contradict such beliefs! This is what their politicians say it's good for the economy, what the media says it's good for the economy, what your school teacher says it's good and what your university professor will say it's good. *It's a massive brainwash* of fiat thinking, Keynesian-based economics and collectivism, all while we're being told that we're winning...

1.39 THE 'PARTIDO LIBERAL LIBERTARIO'

On November 19th 2023 Argentinians elected the first ever self declared 'liberal libertarian' president in world history. I chuckle every time I hear president Milei self declare himself as 'Liberal Libertarian' because that is a term we had to come up for legal reasons with a group of friends on the basement of Cafe *'Petit Colon'* in Buenos Aires in 2009 when we were building the first libertarian political party of Argentina, the "Partido Liberal Libertario'.

We had all met on a Facebook group, we were complete strangers to each other at first and we decided Argentina needed a classical liberal/libertarian party. Back then the world liberal was used as an insult, plain and simple, a derogatory term. So it was really daring for somebody 'to come out of the closet' and mention he was a liberal. Remember that liberal in Argentina does not mean what liberal means in the United States, we are talking about classical liberalism here. Some members of the party didn't want to mention we were liberal and we forked ways right from the very beginning, 'Partido Liberal' on one side and 'Partido Federal Republicano' on the other, that eventually became 'Blue Party' and that one failed really soon.

There was a problem though: the law said that no two parties could be called the same and there was a political party from Corrientes province, the first ever political party of all of Argentina's history, that was named Partido Liberal in 1853.

During those days, I had just recently read Rothbard's *Libertarian Manifesto: For a New Liberty* and was selling copies to the party members. When we had to come up with a new name, I proposed, 'Let's just be called the Libertarian Party.' Another party member then suggested, 'Well, we could combine the two words.

And that is how 'Liberal Libertario' was born.

The party did not succeed in the October 2013 elections and ended in early 2014 but it started a sequence of events that led to libertarianism on the rise.

1.40 PRESIDENT JAVIER MILEI - A NEW HOPE FOR ARGENTINA

Javier was just your regular Chicago school economist working as chief economist for 'Corporación America' owned by argentine-arminian billionaire Eduardo Eurnekian. But in 2014 he discovered Austrian economists Ludwig Von Mises and Murray Rothbard and fell down the libertarian rabbit hole. He bought every libertarian book he could find and get his hands on, secluding himself in his home to 'read them all' for days on end. You can hear Javier's recollection of those early days if you search for his talk when receiving the Hayek Award in Germany, 2024.

Soon he started a radio show, appearing in cable TV programs and later being invited to national air TV. His passion and irreverence caught people's attention and the ratings of the programs would soar. He didn't mind insulting people in their face if they were socialist, communist or left leaning.

For Javier a socialist or a politician is just a thief, so why not insult someone that is trying to steal from you or kill you? He ammased a following in social networks reaching upwards of a million followers and during the pandemic decided to run for deputy in national congress. He got 17% of the votes, a shocker to what he calls 'the political caste system'. They were expecting him to get around 5% of the votes.

The rise of libertarianism in Argentina can be seen as a reaction to decades of money printing and decadence but it must truly be attributed to all the proof of work Javier Milei has done to push anarcho-capitalist ideals into the population. A whole decade of proof of work, doing shows, interviews, theater shows, comedy sketches,

43

rallies, free and open economy classes on town's public squares, you name it. Javier put all his effort into it and the results show.

Two years later he ran in the primaries for president and came in first out of all the candidates of all the parties. The media and the politicians were devastated. Now they could not ignore him and had to invite him. He got second place in the presidential elections but since the elections were close enough, according to the Argentine constitution, a rerun of the election had to be done between the first position, oficialist Sergio Massa and Javier. In this 'ballotage' Javier won with a 56% landslide.

Javier claims to be in favour of "monetary freedom", closing the central bank and giving citizens the freedom to choose the currency of the economy. His proposal includes the idea that citizens should be free to use any kind of private money, not just the dollar, but the dollar has historically been the currency of choice in Argentina to safeguard against inflation.

I've had many personal attempts to 'orange pill' him, teaching him about Bitcoin long before he became a deputy but most of the times the conversation fell short after some couple of minutes and he would reply to me: 'Yeah, Bitcoin is private money and I am all-in for *private moneys.*' It always left me wanting to speak more to make sure just as we'll see in the next section of the book why Bitcoin is not just like 'other private moneys'. I wanted to tell him why Bitcoin is not like Ethereum, Solana, etc. Bitcoin is in a league of its own.

Will Javier manage to turn around a ship that's been sinking for the last 100 years? We will have to see. He is fighting the political caste system that sees politics as a way of life, the media and the education system. If he manages to survive the next two years and gets more deputies in the mid-term elections we'll be able to witness a freedom revolution in a country that has been punished by soviet style regulations for the last century.

President	Term
Raúl Alfonsin	1983-1989
Carlos Menem	1989-1999 , *TWO TERMS*
Fernando De La Rua	1999 - 2001
Eduardo Duhalde	2002 - 2003
Néstor Kirchner	2003 - 2007
Cristina Fernandez de Kirchner	2007 - 2015 , *TWO TERMS*
Mauricio Macri	2015 - 2019
Alberto Fernández	2019 - 2023
Javier Milei	2023 - Present

Argentina's president terms since returning to democracy in 1983

1.41 THE PREAMBLE

"We, the representatives of the people of the Argentine Nation, assembled in General Constituent Congress by the will and election of the provinces which compose it, in fulfillment of pre-existing pacts, with the object of constituting the national union, ensuring justice, preserving domestic peace, providing for the common defense, promoting the general welfare, and securing the blessings of liberty to ourselves, to our posterity, and to all men in the world who wish to dwell on Argentine soil: invoking the protection of God, source of all reason and justice, do ordain, decree, and establish this Constitution for the Argentine Nation."

The libertarian revolution ignited is a revolution of consciousness. Argentina will once again become a beacon of hope for all the working men and women who want to inhabit its land, just as stated in the preamble to the Argentine Constitution.

We will have a 'pro-private moneys' and monetary freedom country, and Bitcoin falls right into that.

We will be able to call Argentina a Bitcoin country.

1.42 BITCOIN IN ARGENTINA

Bitcoin gained early traction in Argentina. The first stories revolve around a unique mailing list called EuDemocracia. Others discovered Bitcoin on gaming forums, particularly those of 3Dfx. Gamers quickly realized that when they weren't playing on their PCs, they could use their video cards to mine this new phenomenon called Bitcoin and generate some revenue.

The first meetup was organized in 2012, followed by many more in 2013, which grew in size as Bitcoin reached new all-time highs. By mid-2013, the Bitcoin community in Argentina had already attracted over 200 attendees to its meetups. By the year's end, Buenos Aires hosted the first-ever Latin American Bitcoin conference.

In 2014, Bitcoin found its first physical home in Latin America: EspacioBitcoin, a co-working space and community center that remains open to this day. Following this, the Bitcoin Argentina NGO was established, offering ongoing education programs from 2017 to the present.

In 2018, the Argentine community brought to life the first-ever Bitcoineta, a Bitcoin van traveling through Argentina and Latin America. As of now, there are four Bitcoinetas traversing the globe: one in Argentina, one in El Salvador, one in South Africa, and one for Europe. Another Bitcoineta is in the works for Ghana and West Africa, with more planned to spread the message of Bitcoin worldwide.

In this context I have described, Argentina's national currency has experienced cyclical and evident abuse, leading to disaster and constant devaluations. This was due to socialist policies and reliance on Keynesian models, where printing money was seen as a magical solution to deficits created by countless governments unable to curb spending or find a solution. The adoption of Bitcoin as a store of value offers an alternative that is not subject to political or governmental manipulation.

My country serves as a poignant example of the consequences fiat currency can bring upon a nation. ***Do you wish for yours to tread a similar path?***

In the forthcoming sections, I will delve into the **solution** offered by **Bitcoin**.

2. What is Bitcoin?

2.1 BITCOIN

Bitcoin is the best money humanity has ever had and it being built and monetized this very moment, as you read my words. It is the concrete realization after answering the question: What would an ideal money be and look like? What would you be able to accomplish with it that you can't with the current state of affairs?

Let's start with what an ideal money would be for you. An ideal money would represent your life's work and it would allow you to send that accumulated work through time and space. It would allow you to store your wealth in a private manner; essentially, you could retain it with you, keeping the key literally 'in your head'. Nobody would be able to tell how much you have or don't have. You would have the freedom to donate it to whomever you desired, or you could opt to donate it to all of humanity if you wished.

It would continually appreciate in purchasing power for the rest of time, meaning that if you save it you can buy more products and services in the future than you can today. It would create incentives to work and it would create disincentives to steal. It would bring a more peaceful world.

What are the restrictions reality imposes on us when we want to turn this ideal money into a concrete form?

All of that and more is what Bitcoin is, and I am going to explain to you why in this section of the book.

2.2 COMMON QUESTIONS

Here are some very useful common questions I get asked at my conferences and courses:

Who created Bitcoin?

Bitcoin was created by a single individual or a group of programmers, working under the pseudonym 'Satoshi

Nakamoto'. Nakamoto who published a white paper titled "Bitcoin: A Peer-to-Peer Electronic Cash System" in 2008, outlining the principles of the cryptocurrency. This academic paper was sent to a Cypherpunk mailing list and you can read it at the end of the book. Cypherpunks are coders, cryptographers and mathematicians that believe in privacy and free and open source software. You can also read on the web the CryptoAnarchist Manifesto and the Declaration of Independence of CyberSpace.

Who is Satoshi Nakamoto?

Satoshi Nakamoto is the mysterious and anonymous creator of Bitcoin. Despite various investigations and speculations, Nakamoto's true identity *remains unknown.* Does it matter who he is? *No, it does not matter.* Satoshi created free and open source software, meaning he programmed Bitcoin and gave it away as *a gift to all to use.* This software belongs to the public domain and as we'll see in later sections can be used by anyone, even enemies. So it does not matter if Bitcoin was created by the CIA, by the Russian intelligence, North Koreans or even aliens. The code is open for anyone to see and audit that there *are no privileges, no 'backdoors', no security gaps.* What matters is that Bitcoin is *speech and math.* Bitcoin is just an idea and *ideas cannot be destroyed by bullets.*

How does Bitcoin work?

Bitcoin operates on a decentralized network with no central point of failure, making it resilient to attacks. Transactions are verified by *'miners'* and recorded by a network of computers (nodes) rather than a central authority like a bank in what's called a 'Blockchain'. You can think of Blockchain as a distributed ledger where each node keeps a copy of an accounting book. What is different about this accounting book is that information is only added at the end of the book and all previous history of transactions are there for public review. Once information is added, it is not deleted nor modified, by anyone (we'll see why this is an impossibility in later chapters).

Bitcoin can be bought, sold, and transferred digitally, using cryptographic techniques to ensure security and ownership. I will explain further in the next sections of the book.

How many Bitcoin are there?

Bitcoin has a finite supply capped at 21 million coins. This scarcity is built into the system's protocol and is intended to mimic the scarcity of precious metals like gold. As more bitcoins are mined, the rate of new supply decreases over time until it reaches the maximum cap of 21 million.

What is a 'satoshi'?

A satoshi, or sat, is the smallest unit of Bitcoin, representing one hundred millionth of a single bitcoin (0.00000001 BTC). It is named after Satoshi Nakamoto, the creator of Bitcoin. One hundred million sats constitute a whole Bitcoin.

Is saving in Bitcoin better?

Saving in Bitcoin offers several advantages, including protection against inflation (arbitrary money creation), censorship resistance, portability through time and space and the potential for long-term growth as the network gets monetized. Due to the current volatility it's better to have medium to long term outlooks when saving in BTC. Additionally, Bitcoin provides financial sovereignty, allowing individuals to control their wealth without relying on intermediaries or governments.

How can we use Bitcoins in daily life?

Bitcoin can be used for various purposes in daily life, including online purchases, remittances, investment, transnational payments, micro-payments and peer-to-peer transactions. It's use is becoming increasingly widespread. Some merchants and businesses accept Bitcoin as payment, and there are also Bitcoin debit cards and payment processors that facilitate spending Bitcoin in traditional retail settings.

2.2 THE WORLD DID NOT HAVE MONETARY FREEDOM UNTIL SATOSHI NAKAMOTO

The current monetary system, detailed in the history of Argentina section, is essentially the system that is running all over the world. What differs between Argentina and the Federal Reserve Central Bank or the European Central Bank or other central banks for that matter is just the degree or rate at which they issue new money and devalue and destroy their currencies. Argentina is a junkie dependent on the 'next high' but more and more first world countries are turning to money printing as an escape to their deficit spending and debt problems.

Central banks issue fiat money, money by decree, out of thin air by printing pieces of paper or typing numbers on a keyboard, and magically creating dollars, euros, pesos, etc. A system that is designed to inflate away, constantly losing purchasing power. A system that is imposed by force, through the coercion of the state on the people. Nobody, not even commercial banks, could come up with their own private currencies and compete with the government moneys according to laws and regulations.

This has changed since the day Satoshi mined block 0 of the Bitcoin blockchain. As I will detail in this section of the book, Satoshi was the first person to discover a way to create a system, that by its nature and design, operates out of the control and possibility of reach of governments. Bitcoin runs on its own separate dimension; let's dive in.

2.3 BITCOIN HAS THE LAWS OF PHYSICS AND MATHEMATICS BEHIND IT

"No matter how large the size of the bomb, it will never solve a mathematical problem."

—George Boole, British mathematician and physicist

Bitcoin establishes a system that takes the rule setters outside of the game. The whole point of the Bitcoin ethos is to have a system where rules don't change unless in a case of utmost emergency. Bitcoin takes corruption out of your money. Bitcoin takes the violence out of your money. Bitcoin takes theft out of your money. To understand why, let's first learn about hash functions.

2.4 WHAT IS A HASH FUNCTION IS AND HOW IS IT CRUCIAL TO UNDERSTANDING BITCOIN?

A hash function is a mathematical algorithm. It was not invented by Satoshi. It is used in cryptography and computer science to generate a 'digital signature' or 'fingerprint' of a given set of data. You choose what data you want to hash; it can be text, an image, a movie, a bitcoin transaction, a PDF file or a company database. Anything that can be converted to binary code - that is, zeros and ones - can be hashed.

After selecting the data, you process it through the mathematical hash formula, yielding a single, *unique result*. Fortunately, manual calculation of the formula is unnecessary, although it's possible if desired. This hashing process ensures a consistent and deterministic outcome, regardless of the time or place of computation.

Regardless of their location or the time at which they perform the action, two individuals hashing the word "Hello" *will obtain identical results*. Bitcoin employs a cryptographic hash function (SHA-256 followed by RIPEMD-160), yielding a distinctive string of characters referred to as a **hash**.

If we hash the word "Hello" using the SHA-256 algorithm, we get as a result:

'185f8db32271fe25f561a6fc938b2e264306ec304eda518007d1764826381969'

But if you hash the word 'Hello' without the first capital 'H' and replace it with lower-case 'h', you get:

'2cf24dba5fb0a30e26e83b2ac5b9e29e1b161e5c1fa7425e73043362938b9824'

Notice that 'Hello' and 'hello' have two completely different outcomes. You can try and verify this for yourself by visiting this website:

https://andersbrownworth.com/blockchain/hash

No matter who you are or when and where you are, you will generate the same answer as me for the same input of data.

You can hash something as simple as 'Hello,' or you could hash the entirety of Wikipedia. You could hash the file of a whole movie, a picture of a sunset, or you could hash the entire private database of a Fortune 500 company. The answer is deterministic.

Another thing worth mentioning is that if, for example, after hashing the picture of the sunset, you decide to open the file in a photo editor and change the color of a single pixel, then save the new version of the photo and run it through the hash algorithm, you will get a totally different result. The new hash bears *no similarity* to the previous hash of the unmodified photo. Furthermore, if you send both photos to someone else for them to hash, they will get the same result as you did.

Another important thing to note is that the inputs—meaning the things you can submit as an input to be hashed—are infinite in number. There is no limit to the variety, types, and sizes of the data you can hash. Yet, here is the interesting thing: the total number of possible answers or outputs of the SHA-256 algorithm is limited. The '256' in the name of the function denotes the size of the possible outputs, as in 2 to the power of 256, or 2^{256}.

That equates to this many possible results:

115,792,089,237,316,195,423,570,985,008,687,907,853,269,984,665,64

0,564,039,457,584,007,913,129,639,936

Try finding a needle in that haystack.

This number is estimated to be 100 times smaller than the number of atoms in our known universe. Essentially, it's akin to suggesting that *the total number of possible answers for the SHA-256 hash function is comparable to the quantity of atoms in our universe divided by 100.*

So, it is possible for two completely different things to be hashed and have the same result as an answer in principle, it's just too improbable to happen. Now, try to find those two things. You will most likely spend thousands of years and a considerable amount of the universe's energy to find which two things, when hashed, give you the same answer.

We will soon see how Bitcoin uses the hash function in many instances and for many different purposes.

2.5 YOUR BITCOIN ARE JUST A SECRET - PUBLIC AND PRIVATE KEY CRYPTOGRAPHY EXPLAINED

If you are able to keep a secret, you will be able to keep your Bitcoin. Your Bitcoin, in essence, is nothing more than a secret, i.e.

information that must be kept private. Whenever you see news of someone 'hacking' Bitcoin or when you read about someone stealing Bitcoin, what you are really reading is that somebody gained access to somebody's secret. Bitcoin as a network, as a protocol, and as a system has not been hacked. It has always been individual secrets that were compromised, not the network and Bitcoin blockchain as a whole.

The entire security model of Bitcoin rests on a finite number of possible secrets—a 2 to the 256 exponent, the same number we saw in the 'What is a Hash' section.

So, the total number of possible Bitcoin secrets is:

115,792,089,237,316,195,423,570,985,008,687,907,853,269,984,665,64
0,564,039,457,584,007,913,129,639,936

Whenever you download a *Bitcoin Wallet* to your phone or boot up a *Hardware Wallet* for the first time, your wallet is selecting one random number from that finite universe of possibilities. It's almost as if your phone chose an atom from the universe as your password, noted the ID number for that atom down in memory, and now you have your Bitcoin secret. The entire Bitcoin ecosystem is built on the assumption that no two people will ever choose the same number as a secret when randomly selected. Problems arise when your phone is not truly random, ie. you're using a malicious app that selects numbers from a small pool of possibilities, or you attempt to choose a random number but fail to do so.

This means that you could just as well choose your Bitcoin secret, which we call a Private Key, by simply flipping a coin or rolling dice and writing down the outcome of your flips or rolls. To understand what is going on inside your Bitcoin wallet app when it generates a private key for you, just grab a coin and designate Heads as '1' and Tails as '0'.

You flip the coin 256 times in a row and you write down the outcome:

11111110000000110111111110011101001101111100110001000111101111101
00100110101010100111111101101101101111100101010011000111100100000101110
10100000001011100111001110111101101101101101110111101101010100110011110110
0101100111000110111110111000100110111011101101100001110

This binary code can actually be translated to a specific natural number. If all the atoms in our universe can have a unique identifying number, then you have effectively chosen one particular atom as your password. Hold on to that number.

No one, not even yourself, will be able to flip a coin again and get the same sequence of heads and tails. This fact *protects the entire Bitcoin economy*. Now that we have generated a *unique personal secret*, Bitcoin software can deduce what the public key and your Bitcoin address are to receive BTC. Using the hash function we learned in the previous section, we can deterministically calculate the public key for any given private key. It's like calculating your bank account number from your password. Choose another password/secret and your bank account number/bitcoin address will change. Want to spend a few coins from your bank account number? Then you better have your secret available somewhere; otherwise, those coins *will be frozen forever*.

2.6 IF YOU HAVE BTC IN AN ADDRESS AND YOU LOSE YOUR PRIVATE KEY, YOU LOSE ACCESS TO YOUR BTC, *FOREVER*.

Nobody will be able to help you, not the police, not the justice system, no government, no Bitcoin foundation, no Bitcoin company, not even Satoshi himself if he so came back. Bitcoin demands of you the **responsibility** of keeping a secret if you choose to use Bitcoin.

You may feel uncomfortable with the responsibility of safeguarding your Bitcoin private key, and in that case, you can delegate that responsibility to someone else. This is how Bitcoin banks, exchanges, or custodial wallets have emerged—examples of BTC holdings where the keeper of the secret to your coins is someone else. However, you become entirely dependent on that third party, if they choose not to return your coins, they won't. They might even claim, 'Oops, sorry, I lost your secret,' or 'Oops, sorry, someone hacked me and stole the coins.' There's little recourse for users of these services, as there's no way to prove whether the key holder institution or actor didn't steal the bitcoins themselves. The crypto world's history is rife with tales of hacks, poorly designed wallets, exchanges being compromised, CEOs passing away and taking customers' private keys with them, and projects disappearing with customer funds. The list is so far and endless that I cannot reproduce it here. I can only suggest that you adopt this Bitcoiner mantra as part of your culture and behavior:

'NOT YOUR KEYS, NOT YOUR COINS'

If you're not taking responsibility for holding your own secrets, don't be surprised when and if you trust someone else to hold your secrets for you and the funds get lost.

2.7 WHAT IS MINING?

Why did Satoshi put this *supposedly inefficient and CO2 producing* mechanism called mining to produce blocks? What did he set out to do and why?

The answer lies in Satoshi's attempt to replicate the same physical constraints of the real world in the digital realm. Prior to Satoshi, all digital information could easily be copied and pasted—it was all just a collection of zeros and ones that could be perfectly replicated with almost no cost. The only way to control access to or modify information was to introduce a central authority and control—an owner of the zeros and ones, acting as a gatekeeper restricting access.

Satoshi envisioned Bitcoin as something you had to earn through effort. It stands in stark contrast to fiat currency, which often seems to offer something for nothing. In this sense, Bitcoin mirrors the characteristics of gold and oil. If you want to own gold, you must either work for it, purchase it from a store, or take the risk of mining it from a mountain with a pick and axe. At the time of this writing, one ounce of gold (31.1 grams) is worth about $2,000 or more than 6 million satoshis. So, if you had to guess, do you think it would cost you less than $2,000 in equipment, time, expenses such as food and lodging, etc., to get a piece equivalent to 31.1 grams of pure gold from a mountain? Chances are that attempting to do so would cost you many multiples of that amount. That is why it is often more practical to visit local gold dealers and buy the shiny certified metal from them.

2.8   BLOCKCHAINS & BLOCKCHAINS

But what exactly are these blocks that we are mining?

You can think of a block as a group of Bitcoin transactions that are audited by a miner, who then puts his seal of approval on the transactions included in the block. This approval signifies that the transactions are valid and can therefore be included in the Bitcoin accounting book (blockchain). These blocks are issued on average every ten minutes and are sequentially numbered. First, we had Block 0, then Block 1, then Block 2, and so on...

For this task, the miner receives a monetary incentive. The miner gets all the fees that people have paid when sending out their transactions plus whatever is the current 'Block Reward.' The Block Reward consists of newly issued BTC, coins that were not in existence/ circulation prior to that block being mined.

Initially, blocks rewarded miners with 50 fresh new BTC, and Satoshi included a 'halving of reward mechanism' in the code whereby every 210,000 blocks (roughly 4 years of time) this BTC inflation gets halved. So on Block #210,000 in the year 2012, the newly created coins per block fell from 50 to 25. In Block #420,000, it halved to 12.5 new BTC per block. The reward was 6.25 BTC for blocks between #630,000 and #839,999, and now we are producing 3.125 new coins for every new block since we are past Block #840,000.

Some people like to call these periods of 210,000 blocks 'an epoch.' As of this writing, we are living in Epoch 5 since we've already been through four halvings of the Block Reward.

Now that we've understood what a block is and why miners are incentivized to produce them, to work really hard for their issuance, we can go deeper into what makes a blockchain different from any other form of database or account registry: this form of storing information only allows you to add information at the end of the accounting book. New blocks can only be added; the past blocks and the information contained in them are not modifiable.

Each block has its own identifiable number and its own unique hash number that serves also as a way to identify it and to prove that the included information is part of that block. Change a comma, a number, remove a transaction, or add a transaction that was not there, and when you hash all the new information, you will not get the same hash. This allows us to personally check that a block is correctly made and complies with Bitcoin rules.

Now we get to the reason why it's called a Block-Chain: The identifying hash of Block #625,427 serves as a required piece of data for the creation of the next block, #625,428. If you haven't built #625,427, you cannot do #625,428. And the final hash of Block #625,428 is dependent on what the previous hash is. Blocks are concatenated with each other, and thus, the resulting hash of a given block is dependent on what happened in all the previous blocks.

Let's say a malicious actor wants to come in and change some information; it could be anything, from audit #490,832. Let's say that someone from Russia sent someone in North Korea 10,000 BTC, and that this 'attacker' wants to change this information, censoring the transaction by removing it from the block as if it had never happened. In order to do that, the attacker would need to rewrite the block without including that transaction. However, since the whole block needs to have its own hash calculated as its identifier, the resulting hash will be different from the block hash it had before the censoring of the transaction. Since the hash of Block #490,832 is a requisite piece of information for the creation of Block #490,833, inputting the newly modified hash from the censored history of the block into the next block introduces a modification into Block #490,833, which invalidates the work that had been done for Block #490,833.

In essence, everything breaks down after Block #490,832 when you try to modify something. Every block is linked to the next one through the inclusion of 'the previous hash' as a requisite. This brilliant idea has turned what could be isolated pieces of audit into a chain that needs to be in perfect order for it to be valid. Change a comma in a block, and you invalidate all the audits that come after that block. All the alarms are set off; there is something wrong, invalid, and that chain is not a valid chain.

This characteristic has made blockchain different from all previous forms of databases. The database of your bank, where your dollars or euros are being recorded, can be edited by someone. The balance can be updated, confiscated, seized, hacked, etc. Not in the Bitcoin blockchain. Past blocks are read-only. The information is public for everyone to see and read, but if you want to update a balance—i.e., send BTC to another address—you need to have the private key, build a transaction, send it to the network, and that transfer of coins will be recorded in one of the next few blocks. The past, where those coins have been, remains unchanged. Information is only added at the end of the accounting book, never modified.

Thus, Satoshi has created the most secure store of information the world has ever had, the most immutable, the most uncensorable there is.

2.8 A THOUGHT EXPERIMENT - OUR OWN FAKE BITCOIN BLOCKCHAIN

Let's imagine for a few minutes that we have a group of people for an experiment. There are 100 participants, and we all download the Bitcoin software. However, instead of becoming regular users, nodes, or miners, we decide to form a private internet among ourselves. In other words, we create what is called an 'Intranet'.

After setting up this private internet connecting the 100 participants, we disconnect it from the real internet, isolating ourselves on our private island of information. Now, we start running our Bitcoin software. Since this software cannot sync up with the nodes of the real internet, all it sees are the computers of the other participants.

Our computers ask the fellow computers, 'Can you pass me the blockchain history?' To which the rest of the computers reply, 'There is no history.' And so, a new blockchain with a *new history* can begin from scratch. Our computers start mining blocks—Block 1, Block 2, Block 3—and with each subsequent block, new bitcoins are created, 50 new BTC per block. Since there are many participants in the network, many people begin accumulating a significant number of Bitcoins, perhaps in the thousands. Our own computers are responsible for all the mining, and we start competing with each other to see who can mine the most blocks and, therefore, earn the most bitcoins. Additionally, we can begin sending BTC between our wallets, *creating a whole history* of transactions.

This experiment of our own fake Bitcoin network can continue for weeks, months, or even years. But to prove the point of the whole story, of the entire experiment, we decide to connect our intranet to the real internet. We want to see what's out there. Immediately, all of our nodes, our Bitcoin software, recognize that there is *another history of events*—a history with *more accumulated blocks* and, fundamentally, a history with more work accumulated within each one of these blocks. The amount of accumulated work is something that can be calculated by checking the hashes of each block.

Our computers then follow...

2.9 THE TRUTH IN THE BITCOIN BLOCKCHAIN

Keep this in mind:

The *truth* is the chain with the **most accumulated work**

Our computers can now compare the two versions of the blockchain, and the story of our little experiment with 100 people and 100 computers doing mining pales when comparing it to the real Bitcoin blockchain, with orders of magnitude more work accumulated. The difference is abysmal... Our computers will then proceed to *discard everything* we have done during the entire extensive experiment. All that accumulated balance, all our experimental fake-Bitcoin holdings, all our transaction history, all the records of all the blocks... it all *disappears in an instant...* as if it never happened.

That is why since its conception Bitcoin has been on a race to add more hashing power.

2.10 THE ALIGNMENT OF INCENTIVES OR HOW BITCOIN IS BUILT FOR ENEMIES

Satoshi found a way to coordinate people and entities to cooperate toward a common goal. Through the correct incentives, he made the existence of the Bitcoin blockchain possible, running perfectly since its launch. Anyone can join the network, anyone can leave the network; there is no network police granting or denying access to read the blockchain, publish a valid transaction, or write a new valid block. Satoshi ensured that it's most profitable, it's in the selfish interest of each participant to abide by the rules of the protocol. Trying to cheat only results in lost money. That same effort, directed towards complying with the protocol, yields a profit. This simple choice between losing and earning satoshis is what has kept the blockchain running. Selfishness is converted into service to others, and cheating and theft are not rewarded.

In this sense, we cannot know if, at this very moment, a dictator in Venezuela is mining Bitcoin alongside the CIA, the Russian Mafia, or the Chinese Communist Party. Enemies in the real world behave like gentlemen in the Bitcoin blockchain. Bitcoin is neutral—the most neutral money there has ever been. All adversaries can join the network and use a common currency that is not controlled by any party.

2.11 BITCOIN'S IMMACULATE CONCEPTION

Bitcoin is the most fair money there is. Satoshi announced Bitcoin by publishing the white paper on a mailing list on October 31st, 2008. He provided the world with advanced notice before officially launching the network and blockchain on the Genesis Block number zero on January 3rd, 2009. To prove that the chain started on that day and not before, he included the title of a newspaper from the day, 'The Times Chancellor on the brink of second bailout to banks'. From that moment on, anyone could participate and join the network. Bitcoin began with the first 50 new bitcoins of the Genesis Block, and anyone could download the Bitcoin software and start mining 50 new bitcoins per block. Satoshi gave everyone an equal opportunity to participate. This stands in stark contrast to most coins launched today, where the 'leaders of the coin' issue coins out of thin air and assign a fair share for themselves.

2.12 BITCOIN IS SLOW ON PURPOSE

Many argue, '*But Bitcoin is old technology! It can only handle 7 transactions per second. Visa can handle 10,000!*' This is true. Bitcoin can only process a handful of transactions each second, but this limitation is deliberate and purposeful, not a technical flaw or an outdated design. We Bitcoiners intentionally choose to have low throughput. The idea behind the Bitcoin blockchain is to create a public, immutable, and uncensorable ledger for eternity. Imagine if we were to write 10,000 transactions each second instead of just 7. The size of the database would grow proportionately, reaching thousands or even millions of gigabytes. Your blockchain would become terabytes and petabytes big. One key idea behind decentralization is that the 'lightness' of the Bitcoin blockchain allows most regular computers to have a complete copy of the blockchain, and verify the integrity and validity of all the blocks themselves. In later sections, we will explore how Bitcoin can overcome these self-imposed limitations and become a currency used by millions and billions of people.

2.13 THE BLOCK SIZE WARS

The debate over how many transactions Bitcoin could handle on each block emerged during 2016 and 2017, known as 'The Block Size Wars'. Some people proposed removing the limit of only 1 MB of information per block, initially through a client/software called 'Bitcoin Unlimited'. This proposal meant that Bitcoin would not have a limit on the number of transactions that could be included in each block. It could be 2000, 20,000, 200,000—whatever the miner decided to include. Each transaction would pay a miner fee, covering the cost of hard drive space, internet bandwidth, and other expenses. There would be a market price to accommodate all these costs.

The issue with this model is that in the Bitcoin blockchain, there are nodes responsible for maintaining a copy of the blockchain, verifying its integrity, and relaying information and transactions among nodes, whether they are mining nodes or non-mining nodes. Operating a non-mining node, a regular Bitcoin node, is a purely benevolent and selfless endeavor. These nodes do not earn money from transaction fees or block rewards. If blocks were unlimited in size, the costs of running one of these personal nodes would skyrocket, and only miners would be able to afford to maintain a complete copy of the Bitcoin blockchain on their hard drives.

Fortunately the idea for 'Bitcoin Unlimited' was soon scrapped but it turned into Bitcoin Cash, an upgrade that would multiply by 8 the capacity of each block by turning the capacity from 1 to 8 MB per block. Some famous bitcoiners from that era backed this proposal and so the war began. It was an ideas war with public debates, YouTube debates, on forums, mailing lists, etc.

The beauty of Bitcoin is that it doesn't have a leader. Satoshi gave us way, so that we did not turn to him for advice, guidance or direction. No set group controls the network and that was demonstrated thanks to these block size wars. Miners, node runners, users, exchanges, and payment processors each held their own distinct opinions.

The was a group that also formed around the idea of doing a slight upgrade to just 2 MB, called Segwit 2X. That's when users united under the banner of UASF, User Activated Soft Fork that meant that node runners could signal their intention to be against the Segwit 2X change. Since there are more user nodes than mining nodes it was demonstrated that the node runners have power and the change to Segwit 2X was not made.

The Bitcoin Cash faction did managed to propose the modification and thus the first major fork of Bitcoin was created.

2.14 HARD AND SOFT FORKS

Bitcoin Cash is a hard fork of Bitcoin. A fork in programming refers to the divergence of a software project, making improvements to the code or taking it in another direction. Thus, there is a change in the Bitcoin code, in the protocol, and in the rules, and there are two kinds of them: the soft fork and the hard fork.

A soft fork is a change in the code that remains compatible with previous versions. The Bitcoin community typically chooses this approach when introducing modifications and upgrades to the Bitcoin code. This means that if you are running an older machine with an outdated version of the software, you can still communicate and operate with other network members running more recent versions. A soft fork, for example, could be considered a self-imposed restraint. A typical illustration of this concept is if the maximum speed limit on a highway is 120 km/hr, and everyone chooses to travel at 80 km/hr instead of 120 km/hr. 80 km/hr falls within the 120 km/hr limit and thus does not violate the rule. Similarly, in the context of Bitcoin, a soft fork could involve producing 0.5 MB blocks instead of 1 MB blocks. Soft forks are backward-compatible and often very challenging to create and implement.

The other option is to perform a hard fork. A hard fork involves making incompatible modifications to previous versions of the software. An upgraded computer cannot communicate with a computer that hasn't been upgraded to the new version of the code.

The ethos and culture of Bitcoin is to try to avoid this kind of fork at all costs, except in cases of absolute emergency.

Bitcoin Cash introduced a hard fork, causing all computers that didn't adopt the new rules to become incompatible with those that did. As a result, the history of the blockchain was split. Bitcoin and Bitcoin Cash share the same common history up until the day of the fork, August 1, 2017. After that day, all blocks and transactions diverged, transactions became different, leading to irreconcilable differences between the two chains.

I remember the day of the fork and the preceding hours very well. Many wondered what would happen to the Bitcoin price. Would it be split evenly between the two coins? And then, would it rapidly move towards one or the other? What ended up happening was that the price of Bitcoin remained relatively stable, while this new coin found its own price. If you held Bitcoin before the fork, it meant that you now had those Bitcoins in two different chains, each with its own price. It was as if new money had come for free. However, what wasn't free was the marketing campaign that the defenders of Bitcoin Cash have been running ever since, trying to claim that they are the real Bitcoin, Satoshi's vision for what Bitcoin is supposed to be. This has led to confusion among newcomers, who may mistakenly believe that they are buying the unmodified Bitcoin when, in reality, Bitcoin Cash today is worth only around 1% of what Bitcoin is worth. Bitcoin Cash, known by the abbreviation BCH, has been a spectacular failure.

It spawned a whole new fashion of creating Bitcoin forks, such as Bitcoin Gold, Bitcoin Private, Bitcoin Diamond, Bitcoin proof of stake. All larger failures than BCH. Even the BCH guys could not contain their hard fork ethos and began fighting and splitting among themselves into smaller and smaller forks.

2.15   HOW IMMUTABLE IS THE BITCOIN CODE?

Therefore we come to a very important conclusion. The way to keep Bitcoin as Bitcoin, to have the finitude of the 21 Million coins and the predictability of monetary expansion, lies in the fact that the *rules remain unchanged.* This is part of the backbone of the Bitcoin ethos. If you want to consider yourself a Bitcoiner, you have to defend this principle. Bitconers don't compromise on this ethical principle. We have all the rest of the fiat currencies and alternative cryptocurrencies for that. It's not a democracy. Bitcoin is a belief system, and we can defend it by resisting changes to the core values of Bitcoin. If a group of people wants to have 100 million coins, they can hard fork Bitcoin and create their own network with 100 million coins. If they want to have an unlimited supply of coins and be just like fiat currency, let them have their Bitcoin Fiat. The beauty of this is that they won't be able to force you to upgrade the software. We can preserve the immutability of Bitcoin as long as we, the Bitcoiners, maintain this Bitcoin *ethos*. Let the proponents of fiat currencies have their own Bitcoin Cash, Ethereums, and so on.

2.16 WHAT IF QUANTUM COMPUTERS ARISE?

Some people are concerned about the possibility of quantum computers emerging in the future, capable of performing calculations that could potentially break the SHA-256 hashing algorithm. Whether or not this day arrives remains to be seen. However, if it does occur, quantum computers would pose a threat not only to Bitcoin but also to the security of banks, governments, utilities, and other entities.

One potential solution to this problem is to upgrade the protocol to use the SHA-512 function. At first glance, it may seem that 512 is simply double the size of 256, but that's not the case. Remember, we are dealing with exponents here. So, while SHA-257 would indeed be double the size of SHA-256, SHA-258 would be quadruple, and so on.

What does it mean to have 512 instead of 256? Recall when I mentioned that 2 to the power of 256 is nearly equal to the number of atoms in the universe.

An analogy I often use is to imagine that having a SHA-512 function is akin to each atom in our universe containing within it another universe of equal size. So, if a quantum computer were attempting to calculate all possible answers, it would need to navigate through our universe's atoms. It would start by examining the first atom, only to find another universe inside it. The quantum computer would then need to calculate all the atoms within that miniature universe before moving on to the next atom in our universe, which also contains another universe within it. This process would continue indefinitely for each atom in our universe...

Here is the total number of 2^{512} according to Wolfram Alpha:

13.407.807.929.942.597.099.574.024.998.205.846.127.479.365.
820.592.393.377.723.561.443.721.764.030.073.546.976.801.87
4.298.166.903.427.690.031.858.186.486.050.853.753.882.811.9
46.569.946.433.649.006.084.096

There are two possible scenarios of quantum computers coming online. One scenario involves one party, being this a company or a government, developing the technology and keeping it to himself without the rest of the world having the same access to the quantum computing technology. This is the worst scenario possible. Remember how the truth of the Bitcoin blockchain is defined as 'The chain with the most amount of accumulated work'. If somebody comes with this technology and starts mining he could develop a majority of hashing power, dominate the issuance of new blocks and censor transactions. Bitcoiners would have to come up with some sort of mechanism to circumvent this attack. The outcome of such an attempt is still open.

The second, more positive, scenario is one in which quantum computers start to gradually come into use and not by just one actor but by many in a decentralized way. If this happens then the incentives of how Bitcoin is designed make it so it's more profitable to put those computers to work in Bitcoin mining than instead trying to use them to try to hack someone's bitcoin secret. In this scenario we would see the rise in computing power rise progressively and it will give us time to ponder if a more difficult hashing algorithm is required.

2.17 BITCOIN'S BLOCKCHAIN AS THE MOST IMMUTABLE LEDGER EVER CREATED FOR MANKIND

Satoshi has bestowed upon us the most secure database we have ever devised. It stands as a public and open registry of information, welcoming participation from anyone. Individuals can access the information, verify its accuracy, and those creating valid Bitcoin transactions can perpetually contribute new data to this record for eternity. What Satoshi has given us is the most difficult-to-alter database in the world. Other common databases used by governments, banks, and corporations are modifiable. Someone with root access (be it the owner, administrator, or hacker) to the database could manipulate the data and alter the rules governing it. Another issue with this model is that someone can be hacked or impersonated, resulting in the modification, alteration, or deletion of all the data within the database. Satoshi has provided us with a public record where we can input new information, ensuring it remains preserved for the entirety of the blockchain's history. Even the most powerful governments and malicious organizations are unable to alter a data point once it has been included in a Bitcoin block.

In every Bitcoin transaction, there exists an open text field known as the OP_RETURN. This field enables the inclusion of short text, such as "I love Mary," or the proof of existence of a certain piece of data at a particular time. What the blockchain cannot do is check the veracity of such a claim or piece of data. I may write forever that I love Mary, but that could be a lie. The temperature of the meat product passing through a supply chain could be a lie as well. You can write truth or lies in the Bitcoin blockchain, forever. Once information is recorded within a Bitcoin block, it becomes immutable. Neither Mary nor anyone else can alter or erase the message, even if she dislikes it. If you later decide to retract your love for Mary, you can only add a new message to the Bitcoin blockchain stating, "I no longer love Mary." That's the extent of what can be done.

The Bitcoin blockchain is the most uncensorable, neutral, unmodifiable, and incorruptible record in human history, and that is a very powerful thing. You can use it to prove that something existed at a certain point in time. You can introduce plain text, but if the information is large, you can introduce a condensed version of your information—its identifiable signature, or a *hash* of the information. Introducing *hashes* instead of plain text on the blockchain has the advantage of protecting sensitive information. Curious onlookers can't determine what the hash represents; only the person with the original data and the hash can decipher it. This person can then choose with whom to share the details behind the *hash*.

2.18 A KNOWN AND PREDICTABLE ISSUANCE & SELF INTERESTED MINING

The current block subsidy as of this writing in 2024 is 3.125 BTC per new block. Every 210,000 blocks this block reward, as a monetary rule set by Satoshi from the get-go, gets halved in half. During the first phase it was 50 BTC per block, then on block 210,000 it got cut to 25 BTC per block, then in block 420,000 it got to 12.5 BTC per block and it is now currently at 3.125 BTC per block since block 840,000. Once we reach block number 1,050,000 it will cut to 1.5625, and to 0.78125 in block number 1,260,000, roughly by the year 2032. If you are able to secure 0.78125 BTC in 2024 you will have the same amount of BTC as miners will get as a whole per each block less than 8 years from now.

Satoshi modeled the system to include miner fees, which are the amounts collected from each entity sending a BTC transaction as a tip for the miners. This 'tipping of the miners' determines the speed at which your transaction gets audited and processed. Miners are selfish entities that try to earn as many satoshis as possible, so they choose from the *mempool*—storage space for unconfirmed transactions within each blockchain node in the network— those transactions that are most attractive in terms of fees.

There have been blocks in the past where the miner fees added up to a higher value than the block subsidy of newly created coins. Eventually, this will occur more frequently until most blocks are created with higher fee amounts than the bitcoin inflation of the total supply. Now, the big questions on the minds of many around the world are: Will miner fees suffice to pay for the whole global mining infrastructure? How much will you pay to include a Bitcoin transaction? My prediction is that it will be similar to the amounts we are paying today when denominated in satoshis, not in dollar terms.

Let's imagine a one million dollars Bitcoin price. Each sat then is worth about 1 penny. If we have 1000 sats as a tx fee that means that the fee will be equivalent to paying 100 USD to move money around. If you can include around 2700 transactions per block, that amounts to a reward of around 2.7 Millions satoshis per block or 0.027 BTC per block. Remember that the current average transaction size for a Bitcoin transaction is moving around 0.4 BTC around or 40 million satoshis. That average transaction will be around 400,000 USD. Paying a 1000 satoshi fee to move 40 Million is a good price to access the most secure and decentralized payment network. Paying the equivalent of 100 USD for moving 400,000 USD.

What will happen when the block reward, that is, the amount of newly created bitcoins in each block that serves as incentive for the miners to sustain the safety of the Bitcoin blockchain halves to insignificant numbers? Let's delve a little into this assumption.

How much budget does the Bitcoin network need to maintain the security of the blockchain and fend off attackers? The exact number is unknown, but some liken it to the budgets of military expenditures of sovereign nations They propose figures around 3%, 2%, 1%, or even as low as 0.5% of a country's GDP. Do we need 3% or just 0.5% of Bitcoin's market capitalization to be consumed by mining infrastructure?

We cannot determine that a priori. All we can estimate is that when Bitcoinization happens, big bitcoin holders will be interested in securing their investment. It doesn't matter if it is a tech entrepreneur, a hedge-fund, a Bitcoin exchange or a sovereign government that has adopted the Bitcoin standard for its treasury. If the miner fees do not suffice for an appropriate level of security I predict *selfish mining*. This means that it will be in the best interest of the biggest Bitcoin holders to start mining, not just to guarantee a sufficient number of hashes per second to deter attacks on the network but also to guarantee the decentralization of the network.

Bitcoin is a network that anyone can use and your best interest is to use it and to keep it decentralized. You have sovereign nations holding bitcoin funds to join the hash race, the race that Satoshi started and cannot end. You decide as a big holder how much of your stack you decide to invest to secure the network as a whole. This is what I call selfish mining, in the interest of securing your portion of the bitcoin network, you are securing everyone's portion.

2.19 THE HASH RACE

Satoshi initiated the hash race, and now it cannot be halted. More hashing power will need to be continuously added to the network for the rest of time. This doesn't mean that Bitcoin will consume the planet's resources or all the energy of the universe. No. What it means is that only a part of our energy consumption will be dedicated towards securing the economic value of all the participants. It just needs to be enough to deter attackers from trying to benefit from using energy to attack bitcoin. One advantage of this scheme is its superiority over past realities, where primary economic value lay in land, incentivizing conquests and wars. Today, economic value is encapsulated in information; it can be represented by a private key, which can be concealed wherever information can be hidden.

This new reality will change the nature of war; it will be uneconomic to get land through war, as land will be much less valuable relative to what Sats can grant you. Land and real estate will be demonetized, along with the value currently held in stocks and bonds; all wealth will flow towards the best-performing asset: Bitcoin, the prime real estate of the digital domain and the cornerstone of the world economy.

2.20 LIGHTNING NETWORK

The 'Lightning Network' is a 'second-layer protocol' proposed as a solution to the self-imposed constraint of the block size limit. It enables Bitcoin transactions to be conducted, without every transaction being recorded on the Bitcoin blockchain, while still providing certainty of payment. Users can create secure payment channels between each other.

To explain how the Lightning Network works, I will first discuss a foundational technology that was available in Bitcoin before the Lightning Network existed: 'Payment Channels'.

2.21 PAYMENT CHANNELS

Payment channels enable two Bitcoin nodes to open a payment channel between them. In this setup, User A would open a channel with User B and allocate a specific amount of Bitcoin between them. I'm going to give two examples so that this can be better understood. Imagine you go to a bar, and this bar sells beers for Bitcoin.

To simplify the math each beer sells for 0.1 BTC. You plan on drinking many beers tonight and are not quite sure how many you'll drink, but you do know for sure that you don't want to pay miner fees each time you order a beer. So, you come up to the owner of the bar and you tell him, *"How about we open a payment channel? I'll put aside one whole bitcoin between my address and your address, and then we can start discounting from there"*. The bar owner agrees, and so you make a Bitcoin transaction that holds the amount of BTC you had between your address and his address. You pay your miner fees, and you can see the transaction on the Bitcoin blockchain. The owner of the bar can also do the same.

Then you tell the barman, *"I want a beer, please"*. The barman replies, *"That'll be 0.1 BTC"*. You say, *"Okay"*, but instead of making a typical 0.1 BTC transaction broadcasted to the whole network, you just create a digital signature using your phone. This creates a valid transaction where 0.1 of that whole bitcoin you set aside between the two addresses is now assigned to the address of the bar owner, and 0.9 remains assigned to your address, that's the remaining change after deducting 0.1 from 1. Even though this transaction was not broadcasted online, the bar owner can check the validity of the transaction by themselves.

Only the owner of the private key could manage to produce a valid signature, sending 0.1 in one direction and 0.9 as a return. The bar owner rests satisfied, knowing that if he wanted, he could broadcast the transaction to the Bitcoin network and have the channel closed, with 0.1 assigned to his address and 0.9 assigned to you as change. Feeling assured by the technology, he then passes you a cold bottle of beer.

You drink it and then ask for another one. "*Sure, no problem*" he says, "*just send another digital signature authorizing a payment*". This time, the transaction is for 0.2 going to the bar owner and 0.8 returning to you as change. You drink your beer and ask for another one. Now you make a digital signature for 0.3 and 0.7, and so on.

This could continue until you have drunk 10 beers, and the entire Bitcoin is assigned to the address of the bar, leaving none for you as change. However, let's imagine that instead of spending the entire Bitcoin, after six beers, you become really drunk and decide to leave the bar with a suspicious-looking lady.

The bar owner doesn't require anything from you; he just takes the latest digital signature you provided him and sends it to the Bitcoin blockchain to close the payment channel. Miner fees are paid, and the balance is settled: 0.6 BTC goes to the address of the bar, and 0.4 BTC returns to you as change. Despite there being six different payments during the night, the Bitcoin blockchain only saw two payments: the opening and the closing of the payment channel. Between the opening and the closing, there could have been hundreds, thousands, even millions of payments among the two participants if they chose to do so. These payment authorizations are private, instant, and costless. You are only constrained by what your two computers can handle.

This is a summary of how payment channels work. It's a technology that has been available in Bitcoin for years but went mostly unused.

2.22 BACK TO THE LIGHTNING NETWORK

In early 2016, Joseph Poon and Thaddeus Dryja published a white paper announcing the idea to create the 'Lightning Network' as a scalable off-chain instant payments solution to the scalability constraints of the Bitcoin blockchain. They proposed to create a network of payment channels that connected entities and routed payments.

Example:

Alice opens a Lightning channel with Bob and contributes 1 whole BTC to the channel. This transaction is recorded on the blockchain and pays miner fees. The Lightning channel allows them to send and receive BTC among themselves until they decide to close the channel by broadcasting a transaction that settles the final balance, also paying miner fees. Between the opening and closing of the channel, they could have conducted dozens, hundreds, or even thousands of transactions among themselves, none of which were ever recorded on the Bitcoin blockchain, saving time and fees.

Now let's imagine that Bob opens another channel with 59 million sats (0.59 BTC) with Carter, and Carter had previously opened an 11 million sats channel with Maria. What the Lightning Network enables is the ability to find routes and connections among users. So, if Alice wants to send her sats to Maria, she can do it by routing the payment through Bob and Carter.

It works like this: Alice tells Maria she wants to pay her one million sats through Lightning. Maria opens her Lightning wallet app, and the app generates an "invoice" for one million sats in the form of a QR code. This QR code allows Alice's app to start looking for a route to get to Maria. Fortunately, there is one available through Bob and Carter.

At the moment Maria creates the invoice to receive payment, her app also generates a secret that only she will keep for now. This secret is stored within the memory of the app; Maria doesn't need to see the secret for this to function. Alice's app finds a route and creates a package that will be sent to Bob. This package is built in layers, so Bob receives it and, using his private keys, he can unlock a layer, like peeling an onion, and see that Alice is assigning him a little over one million sats, and that the next destination of the package is Carter. This transfer has shifted the balance in their channel. At first, Alice had one million sats in her name and now has authorized Bob to be the owner of those sats. But if Bob wants to take his routing fee, he has to assign some of his sats to Carter. Lastly, Carter sends one million sats to Maria and is able to collect his routing fee.

Remember that Alice and Bob had previously opened a channel amongst themselves that held one whole Bitcoin. The balance in this channel could have been distributed in any way; Alice owning the Bitcoin, Bob owning the Bitcoin, or somewhere in between like 60% for Alice and 40% for Bob. If they started with a balance of 60 million sats in Alice's favor and 40 million sats for Bob, this new transaction updates the balance between them.

Now, Alice's balance is 59 million sats, and Bob's balance increases to 41 million sats. Bob then takes the package and redirects it to Carter. Bob sees the package coming from Alice and he sends it to Carter but he doesn't know about the final destination, Maria. Now Carter can open the package with his private key and see there is a one million sats transfer to Maria so his balance with Bob increases by a million and his balance with Maria decreases by a million. Maria unlocks the last package with her private key and finds the one million sats payment that originated with Alice.

Maria can only see that the payment came routed through Carter, her only connection in the lightning network. In order to definitively claim the million sats for herself she needs to reveal to everyone on the chain the secret that the app had chosen at the moment of the creation of the invoice. This revealing of this secret is what guarantees Alice that the million sats effectively reached Maria and were not lost/stolen in the way. The only way for each connections balance to adjust to the new values is for everyone to be able to do it, not just some in the chain.

Now you may ask, why would Bob and Carter volunteer in helping Alice reach and pay Maria? The answer lies in that Bob and Carter have offered their services for a fee. It wasn't free. When Alice's app was trying to find a way to reach Maria the app checked all the possible routes and asked each intervening hop along the way: What is your price if I use you? Each intermediary in the chain of peer connections can choose the price they charge to be used as a routing mechanism. If the price is too high your app can choose a different path.

If there is no alternative available that is the price you will have to pay. If you do not like the Lightning price you might choose to pay Maria through the conventional Bitcoin blockchain with BTC you have outside of Lightning. Sometimes there might not be any path connecting you to someone else.

Another constraint of the Lightning network is that each channel becomes a bottleneck for the amount of money that can be routed inside of it. Carter had opened a channel of only 11 million sats with Maria so if Alice tried to send Maria 21 million sats she would not be able to do so because the last connection needed, the Carter-Maria only has 11 million sats in it. You may read all of this and say, wow, it must be bloody awful and complicated to use the Lightning network but in reality there are apps that simplify all of these.

You don't have to worry about opening channels, choosing how much to put in, putting a price on routing fees, creating secrets, checking that payments really got through, etc. It is all done for you in the background. But if you choose to become a Lightning network power user you can become one and you can open channels with friends, with other bitcoin users, etc.

2.23 WHAT THE LIGHTNING NETWORK ENABLES

Lightning is a truly peer-to-peer solution. Anyone can become a Lightning node, route payments, add liquidity to the network, and earn routing fees in exchange. There is no barrier to entry or exit. Additionally, Lightning offers increased privacy compared to the

Bitcoin blockchain, where all transactions are recorded forever and visible to anyone. Transactions on Lightning remain private among the involved parties.

Lightning is also practically instantaneous, there's no need to wait for block confirmations except when opening or closing a channel. Once you're inside the network, you can send thousands of payments, all clearing instantly. In a sense, you could be sending micropayments every second, making it almost like a streaming of money. The number of transactions per second in the Lightning network is limited only by what the users want and what their computers can handle.

2.24 HASHING POWER IS THE ONLY PROPRIETARY ADVANTAGE

You'll see many coins competing for the latest and shiniest new features like smart contracts, privacy, and more. However, unless any of these coins, such as Ethereum, Solana, Cardano, etc. truly come up with something unique to them that is non-copyable, other coins can simply copy and paste those open-source developments. Since these developments can be copied, they will be copied, and they can even be introduced in upper layers of Bitcoin. For instance, if you want to have smart contracts in Lightning, you can have it. If you want to incorporate more privacy in Lightning, you can have that too. Essentially, there's nothing in the other chains that cannot be copied and adapted within the Bitcoin ecosystem. The only thing that cannot be copied or replicated by any other chain or actor is the accumulated work of the Bitcoin blockchain. That is the only irreproducible element, and we Bitcoiners will continue to defend that unique advantage. While we may copy features developed by other coins, they won't be able to replicate the fortitude of the Bitcoin blockchain.

2.25 SELF CUSTODY

Not your keys
Not your coins

Bitcoin allows you to be sovereign. It grants you the most private form of property beyond your consciousness and individualization. Your bitcoins are the secret you keep in your head, you know how to unlock their transfer to another address. If you lose this secret, you lose your bitcoins; they will still be there in the blockchain, but the fact that you are not able to access them means they are no longer yours. You can choose to give custody of your bitcoins to a third party, such as an intermediary, a bitcoin bank, or a bitcoin exchange. In that case, they will be managing the keys and will be the ultimate responsible "owners" of those bitcoins.

Bitcoin history is plagued with accounts of hacks of exchanges, exchanges going bankrupt and bitcoin companies disappearing with 'customers' funds. Plagued with it. An exchange owner can tell you: 'Oops, we've been hacked. We lost everything, it's gone, we are bankrupt now, sorry…' It will most likely be impossible to prove if he stole the bitcoins for himself. It could be true that someone else stole the BTC but it could also be true that he stole it for himself. There is a mechanism called *Coinjoin* whereby the trail/path of the BTC in the blockchain can get diffused up to a point where you cannot prove without reasonable doubt where they went. Thus the thief will conjoin the coins with other users of the blockchain trying to add privacy to their holdings. *Coinjoin after coinjoin after coinjoin the trace will be lost.*

2.26 THE TEMPTATION TO CREATE YOUR OWN MONEY

Imagine if you had a money printer and you could make all the money that you wanted and needed? How easy and interesting life gets when you don't need to work for money, right? Imagine all that you could do with that money. The temptation is great, it would be like having a cheat code for life.

All throughout recent history, individuals and groups have attempted to gain access to money creation. You could even say that Bitcoiners are attempting the same. However, here's the catch: It's one thing to create money that is essentially free to produce, and another to create money that is extremely difficult to generate. By 'difficult,' I mean money that requires a significant amount of work, investment, time, and risk.

Rome had emperors that provided the market with quality gold coins and Rome also had emperors that surreptitiously melted the pure gold coins to create new coins that included a lesser, cheaper metal inside thus having gold to create a larger quantity of coins. Those emperors were cheating the population and generated inflation, thus stealing people's life energy at a distance.

All recent history has been a dance between hard money creating good times and easy money creating bad times.

This temptation to create money and be in control of it has not ceased.

Ever since Satoshi first introduced Bitcoin, there have been attempts to replicate its success. Some aim to become the next Bitcoin, others strive to be a superior version, while some simply aim to inflate the value as much as possible before cashing out. Essentially, there is a temptation to engage in pump and dump schemes, or to rug-pull. Initially, it was quite simple: just copy the Bitcoin code, tweak a few parameters, and voila! You have yourself a new cryptocurrency in just a few minutes. Thus, the concept of 'Altcoin' was born, and soon enough, Bitcoin enthusiasts began referring to altcoins as 'shitcoins'

People trying to launch new coins soon realized one insurmountable fact about Bitcoin: *it cannot be replicated.*

Satoshi stated in the Bitcoin code that the truth of the Bitcoin blockchain is the chain with the most amount of accumulated work.

That means if I come and decide to create a similar copy of Bitcoin, let's call it ArielCoin. I modify Bitcoin's code, set the total supply to 100 million coins, and now I can launch my new coin. However, to establish my proof-of-work coin, I need to find miners willing to work on my coin's blockchain. For the sake of this argument, let's imagine I am very successful and I convince one thousand miners, or one thousand machines, to hash the ArielCoin blockchain. With this network established, I can start my chain, add blocks, create new coins, make transactions, and pay transaction fees. We could continue with this experiment for days, months, or even longer, until someone decides to attack the ArielCoin blockchain (let's keep it between us; I coordinate the attack myself). If ten thousand machines decide to point their miners towards my blockchain, they can effectively control and manipulate it as they wish. In Argentina, we would say, "*Te la hacen de goma*" (they can turn your blockchain into the most malleable rubber). blockchain technology, in this scenario, offers zero safety. What was so great about it after all, then?

The only thing that protects the Bitcoin blockchain is maintaining its lead in hashing power. Satoshi started a race that cannot be stopped, and as Bitcoiners, we must strive to have the greatest lead possible. It's a hash race, one that is more peaceful than an arms race. The more hashing power the Bitcoin blockchain accumulates, the safer it becomes. All lesser blockchains are more vulnerable to attack and less secure.

2.27 THE REAL REASON WHY PROOF OF STAKE IS BEING PUSHED

The *Cryptobros**, realizing that the proof-of-work hashing mechanism only allows for a few blockchains, needed to find an alternative that would enable them to create new coins more easily. Thus, the consensus mechanism of proof of stake became the predominant choice for launching new coins. In order to market the choice of proof of stake over proof of work, they had to promote it as something that "consumes less energy" or "is better for the environment".

The real reason is because they cannot copy Bitcoin.

Talking about Bitcoin's CO_2 consumption is a means to attack the consensus mechanism they cannot have for themselves. They have to make do with a lesser consensus mechanism.

Cryptobros are individuals within the cryptocurrency community who are known for their enthusiastic attitude towards shitcoins. They also sometimes refer themselves to as 'Degens' for being degenerate with their reckless attitude towards investing.

2.28 WHY PROOF OF STAKE IS A LESSER CONSENSUS MECHANISM

To create a proof-of-stake coin, you first need a leader. This leader can be a charismatic person, a foundation, or a DAO (Decentralized Autonomous Organization, most likely decentralized in name only).

The steps to create a Proof of Stake blockchain

SCENARIO A: Tony the scammer

Pepe comes along and has seen the riches that many people have accumulated in the crypto world. He decides that he will try to promote a new coin with the intention of creating a pump and dump or rug-pulling the investors of the coin. This is his intention from the get-go. He needs to craft a narrative; perhaps the coin will be positioned "for the health industry," or for the "cannabis industry," or as a new decentralized *something*. He begins pitching it to the initial investors, offering them access to the first coins at a discounted price.

Step #1: Tony has to sit down at a computer and inputs the initial supply of coins to be created. In the Bitcoin world, we call this a *premine*. He types in 10 billion units and hits 'Enter'. Suddenly, the first 10 billion coins materialize out of thin air and fall under his control.

Every proof-of-stake blockchain undergoes this unavoidable step. Without coins in existence, there's nothing to be staked.

Step #2: Tony must distribute the coins among users according to some rule, most likely going to the investors who supported the coin when it was still an idea. He sends one billion coins to investor A, two billion to investor B, three billion to investor C, and so on, while retaining a significant portion of coins for himself.

Step #3: The staking can start. Having distributed the coins to many different addresses now the owner of each address can decide how much of the coins to stake. They have the option not to stake, i.e., to have a zero stake. Alternatively, they can choose to stake 10%, 50%, or even 100% of their coins, depending on their preference.

Step #4: The sum of all individual stakes is added up. Let's assume, for the sake of this argument, that a total of 2 billion coins out of the initial supply of 10 billion coins have been put at stake by individual holders. The action of putting the coins at stake is akin to opening a Certificate of Deposit in a bank; the coins get locked up and cannot be used for spending. With 2 billion coins at stake and 8 billion in circulation, this means 20% of the total supply is staked.

Step #5: Now we can start to produce blocks.

If user A has staked 200 million coins, they hold 10% of the total 2 billion coins at stake. Consequently, their computer will be selected approximately 10% of the time to produce a valid block. To propose a new valid block, this computer doesn't need to perform a substantial amount of work; it simply selects the transactions, adds the transaction fees, assigns the newly created coins to the validator's address, and submits the block for all to incorporate into their blockchains. The remaining validators then essentially give a thumbs up or thumbs down to this newly proposed block.

In principle, as long as the block producer follows the rules of the coin, the new block should receive a thumbs up. However, if the block producer cheats or fails to adhere to the coin rules, the block receives a thumbs down and rejection from all other validating nodes. Consequently, the block doesn't get included in their copy of the blockchain. Moreover, as a form of punishment for the cheater, their stake is slashed, confiscated, and redistributed among the remaining validators according to their stake holdings.

Step #6: The 'Rug-pull'. A proof-of-stake blockchain can be maintained as long as nobody controls 50% or more of the stake. If someone were to have over half of the stake, it means that he can give the thumbs down to other validators and reject their blocks and confiscate their stake. Essentially, he can take control of the network.

Some coins even have mechanisms to propose changes to the protocol and core software running the coin. These changes could involve alterations to the coin's supply, adjustments to the consensus rules, and so on. The proposed changes are submitted for a vote, and you can vote in accordance with the stake that you hold.

The issue arises from the fact that most proof-of-stake systems are created out of thin air by a leader, whether that's an individual or a foundation. Subsequently, this leader must 'fairly' distribute the coins by sending them to different addresses. As an observer watching the coins move within the blockchain, it's impossible to ascertain with certainty whether some of these addresses belong to the leader, their business partners, spouse, lawyer, best friends, etc. You can only observe that the coins are distributed among various addresses, but you can never definitively determine the ownership of those addresses.

So, the leader or scammer will undoubtedly claim that the coins and the network are 'decentralized,' when in reality, they may not be, and there's no way to prove otherwise. In a proof-of-stake system, it's impossible to verify whether the coins were distributed fairly or not. Both a benevolent leader and a scammer will make the same assertion: the coins have been distributed, and nobody controls over 50% of them. There's no way to prove or verify this until the day the rug-pull occurs, and you may never even realize it happened. Perhaps scammers might propose changes to the monetary rules and consistently win the elections with changes that benefit them.

2.29 PROOF OF STAKE IS FIAT - THE MOST PERFECT TOOL EVER DEVISED TO SCAM PEOPLE

That's why cryptobros and scammers have begun advocating for proof of stake. It's not because of CO2 emissions or environmental concerns, as they like to say. Rather, it gives them the chance to generate all the coins they desire, effortlessly, at no cost, and in no time. Essentially, proof of stake is simply a new rebranding of the Fiat world. It becomes unknowable whether the leader is benevolent or a scammer until the moment the scamming is realized. If the coin fails, the leader or scammer can attribute it to an attack on the network, a flawed change of policy, a code alteration that underwent a vote, or just bad luck. We tried and it didn't succeed. The issue is that the leader could have voted for themselves and you can't prove it. This is why this system has all the incentives aligned to be the perfect tool for scams, with little incentives to be honest. Scammers using this system get away with it legally, *without facing jail time.* For a non-believer in the private property of others, what more could they ask for? Proof of stake has effectively become fiat, making it the most perfect tool ever devised to *scam people.*

2.30 CRYPTO FASHIONS

The world of cryptocurrencies exhibits *fads*, cycles where a shiny new big thing becomes the trending topic promising to 'revolutionize' everything and offer quick riches to its participants. After many years in the ecosystem, one can observe fads come and go, often leaving a trail of people who have been scammed or ripped off.

Altcoins

Initially, it was the 'Altcoins', alternative coins. Anyone could copy and paste the Bitcoin code, tweak a few parameters, and launch a new crypto-token. However, these projects lacked the mining security of the Bitcoin network. Alternatively, some proposed entirely overhauled codes with different operational mechanisms. After more than 25,000 of these tokens were created, it's safe to say that 99.99% have failed to reach the top spot, and most likely experienced nothing more than a pump and dump scheme that enriched the creators and early investors of the tokens. Consequently, most of these *shitcoins* have died out.

Virtual Machines

Then came the era of Virtual Machine Blockchains. Vitalik Buterin, a young programmer and Bitcoin advocate at the time, proposed a new coin and blockchain that would enable not only the transfer of coins but also the execution of simplified computer programs on the blockchain. Many other cryptocurrencies offer similar features with projects like EOS, Cardano, and Solana. You can read more about this in the Ethereum section of this book.

Bitcoin Forks

A fork occurs when you introduce a change in the code and rules of a software—in this case, the Bitcoin software—and the proposed change is not compatible with previous versions. This incompatibility requires everyone need to upgrade their software simultaneously to to continue operating. In 2016 and 2017, Bitcoin experienced its "Blocksize Wars' where bitcoiners debated whether the amount of data stored in each block should be increased to raise the throughput or number of transactions that can be included in the blockchain. Some believed this change would allow more participants and lower fees for users, thereby reducing revenue for miners.

Bitcoin's long—term survival dependent on miners having adequate fees for their operation, so a roadmap of constantly modifying the fee market—and thus the rules—did not sit well with most of Bitcoiners.

The dissidents created Bitcoin Cash (BCH), a 2017 fork of Bitcoin, which increased the block size from 1MB to 8MB. This led to other forks like Bitcoin Diamond, Bitcoin Gold, Bitcoin Private, and even a Bitcoin with Proof of Stake. None of these have achieved significant relevance. Currently, the value of one BCH hovers around 1% of the value of a Bitcoin.

ICOs

The 2017-2018 ICO (*Initial Coin Offerings*) boom provided anyone an easy way to raise capital by issuing tokens. This led to numerous scams and failed projects, some resembling pyramid schemes where early entrants profited at the expense of later investors, culminating in a burst bubble. Others disappeared outright after the initial token sale.

DeFi

DeFi platforms (Decentralized Finance) recreate financial systems on the blockchain, promising inclusion and transparency. However, they also carry significant risks, such as smart contract vulnerabilities and market manipulation, leading to high-profile failures.

NFTs

Non Fungible Tokens are created to represent something from the real or digital world. For example, Jack Dorsey sold the first tweet on Twitter as an NFT, fetching millions of dollars, even though the token is not actually linked to the tweet except through perceived value. I'd recommend caution, as most investors lose their money.

The Metaverse

It envisions a virtual shared space with blockchain-enabled economies. While it has attracted significant investment, practical development lags behind the hype, posing technical and economic challenges that could disappoint early adopters.

AIs

Most likely the latest fashion for the crypto world in 2024 will involve new tokens to be backed by AI. In reality, while Artificial Intelligence is promising, new tokens are unnecessary for its integration. AI's will be able to hold their own Bitcoin, whether on the Blockchain or through the Lightning Network. We will be able to 'send our AI to work for us' and receive 'pay at the end of the day'.

2.31 WHY THE WORD 'BLOCKCHAIN' IS A BASTARDIZED WORD

Satoshi Nakamoto did not mention the word 'blockchain', even though he invented it. He sometimes referred to it as the 'timechain'. What is the purpose of a blockchain? Anticensorship, antifragility, neutrality. That is the only reason why decentralization is sought after, not because it's an end in itself but for the fact of maintaining the most equitable distribution of power as possible to diminish the chances of an attack. If a Blockchain is not decentralized and the nodes/validators/miners can be identified and attacked, it is susceptible to attack.

In this scenario, would it make sense for a private company to sell a Blockchain solution to five banks for them to have a settlement layer? Let's imagine a three-letter computer company comes along and sells the "SuperLedger" to these five banks. The banks start validating the blockchain in a predefined order. First block is validated by Bank A, Block #2 by Bank B, Block #3 by Bank C and so on and then repeat. They can play this game of 'having a blockchain' for months or even years. Then comes a government like Argentina's and tells them as it happened in 2002: Take all the 'clients' dollar accounts, set the accounts at zero dollars for the whole population and multiply the original amount by 1.4 and add it to the pesos column.

Do you think any of the five banks would come to the government and say, Dear government, we cannot delete the balances! We are using a blockchain! Of course not. A change in the code running the 'blockchain' would be submitted, and all the modifications that you dare to imagine can be incorporated. An example of a blockchain that wasn't really a blockchain. It is not accomplishing its *raison d'être:* to be a neutral, immutable ledger.

Thus, when you see someone touting 'I'm not interested in Bitcoin, I'm interested in the Blockchain', this is a huge red flag. Either this person still has not learned how unsafe crypto blockchains can be or the person is trying to hide behind the jargon, to show off 'as intelligent' or as a concealed plan to scam people.

2.32 MAKE ETHEREUM IMMUTABLE

Bitcoiners like to say that the Ethereum blockchain has never reached the level of blockchain as it has not proven to have the key characteristic a blockchain is trying to achieve: immutability.

First, it was issued by a presale funded by BTC that payed for the writing of the code. The BTC was distributed among the programers meaning that they could anonymously keep buying these cheap Ethereum at 30 cents of a dollar. This is unprovable of course but possible, nothing limited the buying of more tokens with the proceeds of the token sale, essentially creating a financial bycicle or financial loop that benefits the issuers.

Then, after the launch, in 2016 there was a massive project called 'The DAO' for Decentralized Autonomous Organization that gathered people's funds into a Ethereum Smart Contract. Think of a DAO as a 'decentralized' LLC or NGO. This limited liability company is not registered in any particular country, it lives 'on the blockchain'. The goal of The DAO was to, once the subscription was closed, vote on what the DAO should work on or invest in. So, at the time people were sending their Ethereum funds to the project, they had no idea what the eventual use of those funds would be. In total people sent around 150 Million dollars to the smart contract. A hacker or a group of hackers found a vulnerability in the DAO's code (or was it planted there all along by the software developers?) And was able to 'withdraw the dividends' from the DAO. Little by little, everyone could see on the Ethereum blockchain how all the 150 million worth of Ethereum tokens were being siphoned out of the smart contract. This was a catastrophe for the Ethereum community right at the very beginning of the project.

Vitalik and team found a solution that set the culture: they made a change code in the Ethereum software and blockchain to make it so for this robbery to have never taken place. Everybody would have his tokens back in their respective wallets as if the people have never sent them over to the DAO. Vitalik and team effectively became police and judges of the Ethereum blockchain deciding on which hacks needed a hard fork in the code to return funds to their owners and which hacks didn't need such a change. Almost like when Central Banks bail out some banks but not others, sound familiar?

The last straw of why Ethereum is a shitcoin is it's transition into the Proof of Stake validation algorithm and the fact that they introduce changes to the monetary policy every a few months or years. To see why Proof of Stake is a lesser consensus algorithm you can check the dedicated section in this book. Regarding the monetary policy, at first Ethereum did not have a cap or limit on how many ETH could be issued, unlimited cap, just like fiat dollars, euros and pesos.

Then they proposed a change to 'Ultra Sound Money' trying to compete with Bitcoin, as in, if BTC supply is capped at 21 Million, an ever shrinking ETH supply should be better, right? Right? The way they introduced this hard fork chain into the monetary rules was by introducing a new fee on top of the miner/validator fee. This fee is called the burn fee and is supposed to slash that part out of existence, out of the supply. When I saw that I thought to myself: Ohh my, they have introduced a transfer tax! Why is it a tax? Because it punishes people using the network in favor of those that don't move their coins. It makes moving ETH around more expensive and the slash benefits all ETH holders, just like a redistribution of wealth.

In summary, Bitcoiners see Ethereans as just another privately managed project, with a supposedly benevolent king in Vitalik Buterin proposing changes in the economic rules constantly. If people are going to get rug pulled as what happened with other Ethereum imitators is yet to be seen. These behaviors and culture are the opposite of what Bitcoin stands for. In Bitcoin we don't change the rules unless in case of utmost emergency. Ethereum makes a hard fork (incompatible with the past change of rules) every a few months. So it's hard to say what Ethereum is. The real question is what is Ethereum these months?

To go deeper on this controversial subject, I suggest reading the book 'The Infinite Machine' author Camila Russo, *Harper Collins, 2010.*

2.33 WHY BITCOIN AND NOT CRYPTO

The crypto world is trying to latch onto Bitcoin's success, promoting the idea that all cryptocurrencies are safe and futuristic because they use 'cryptography' and 'blockchain technology'. In reality, the ease at which they can be created and the discretionary nature of new cryptos make them as risky and unpredictable as fiat government money, if not worse. Unfortunately, we are still at a stage where many people lump Bitcoin together with other 'cryptos', treating them as if they are the same or directly comparable.

However, the truth is that cryptocurrencies, in general, are much more similar to fiat money than they are to Bitcoin. Bitcoin stands apart due to its 15 years plus of sunk proof of work, it's most decentralized nature, fixed supply of 21 million coins, and established track record since its inception in 2009. As Michael Saylor would put it: 'There's no second best'.

Many new cryptocurrencies, on the other hand, lack these attributes. They are often created with centralized control, can be minted in unlimited quantities, and have not yet proven themselves in terms of security or long-term viability. This proliferation of new, unproven cryptocurrencies contributes to market volatility and poses significant risks to investors, as many of these projects can fail or turn out to be outright scams.

In summary, while Bitcoin has established itself as a unique digital asset with a strong foundation and clear use case, many other cryptocurrencies do not offer the same level of security or reliability. As such, it is crucial for investors to understand the fundamental differences between Bitcoin and other cryptos to make informed decisions.

2.34 SEC PLEASE DON'T BAN CRYPTO - LET'S CHANGE THE CULTURE

Crypto, not Bitcoin, is a new way to issue securities. Anyone can do it, a 14 year old kid can do it, your government can do it, the scammers do it all the time, your AI can do it, you can do it. Some bitcoiners have adopted the position that as issuing securities without regulation is banned in most countries, they are demanding that the Securities and Exchange Commission, the USA organ, or regulator in charge of regulating the issuance of bonds and stocks, regulate the crypto world. I believe this is a terrible idea.

The whole concept of cryptoanarchy is to get freedom back. What we do have to do as bitcoiners is take on the job of educating the public and promote a change in culture where 'Crypto' or 'blockchain' doesn't mean 'safe'. For all the reasons exposed here, it's *far from safe*. But it doesn't mean that somebody couldn't use it in a correct way as long as they desired to remain honest.

That is why I believe the message should be: Crypto is anarchy land, it's the new far west, 'Enter at your absolute own risk'. Know the risks and the easiness by which you can get scammed. Proceed accordingly as you learn and don't be surprised if you get rug-pulled. You knew what you were getting into.

2.35 STABLECOINS - SHITCOINS FOR THE SHORT TERM

In 2014 Tether launched the first stablecoin, the USDT. The idea behind stablecoins is for them to be worth a determined amount of another good and some people like to call them 'pegcoins' as in that they are pegged to something else. This something else could be the US dollar, the Euro, an ounce of gold, a barrel of oil, etc. We could even have representations of stocks and bonds using this token. The big question then becomes: who issues them and how do you guarantee their price peg to the asset? There are multiple ways of achieving this goal, and that is why whenever you are presented with a new stablecoin, you have to investigate its pros and cons in detail.

Let's start by explaining the USDT case to delve into how it works. Tether Limited is an actual company established in a specific country with a CEO, CTO, bank accounts, employees, etc. The model behind the token is that Tether, as a company, will hold either US dollar cash in bank accounts or US Treasury bonds that pay interest on the holdings. As of this writing, the size of the Tether market is upwards of 80 billion dollars, meaning that if all those 80 billion tokens in circulation are backed by US T-Bills paying 5% in interest, Tether as a company is making 4 billion dollars annually just in interest from the US government. That equates to over 10 million dollars a day in revenue, every day. Not bad for a company with fewer than 100 employees.

'Tether is centralized. This is not something that is up for debate' the CEO of the company, Paolo Ardoino, states it so when he gives public lectures. And so are most other stablecoins; we will see the differences shortly. Yet, Paolo is also a hardcore bitcoiner, and thus Tether as a company is buying BTC for its reserves and investments with the interest payments from the US Government. Funny how, thanks to stablecoins, the US Government is financing the purchase of Bitcoin and raising BTC's price.

There is also USDC in the United States, a company started by Coinbase and Circle. Some believe that, since it is under the vigilant eye of the US government, this token is better; others believe it is an inferior token for the same reason. Since these coins are centralized, your coins could actually get frozen on an order from the company.

Stablecoins are a necessary evil on the path of Bitcoin adoption. They provide a more freeing experience to the people holding stables versus having dollars in a bank account. Many people around the world cannot have a bank account. Many people around the world, like the Argentine, don't trust local banks with their dollars, they save in cash. With stablecoins you can have any amount, anywhere in your wallet/private keys.

3. Politics, Economics and Philosophy

3.1 HISTORY OF MONEY

F irst of all, we need to understand *what money is*. Why do we need it?

At one moment in the history of mankind, we were just like any other animal. However, over time, 'this animal' developed abilities that set it apart from the rest of the animals: the ability to reason, to use logic, to develop language, and to start counting—the birth of mathematics.

You may attribute it to continuous evolution or to the act of God but man decided that he did not want to live like the rest of the animals. He sought to improve his condition beyond mere survival and the basic necessities of hunting and gathering food. He aimed to build shelters, develop tools, create clothing for warmth, and establish methods for storing food. In doing so, he discovered economics without even realizing it—he was economizing. That is, he was making decisions about how to best allocate his time. Since his time on Earth is finite, he had to economize his scarcest resource: time. While he could have spent his time hunting with his bare hands, one day he decided not to hunt. Instead, he chose to fast and dedicate his time to building a tool to hunt more efficiently—to achieve the same outcome in less time. By sacrificing immediate hunting time to develop and test a tool—a new technology—he was able to free up his time and multiply the outputs from his inputs, essentially multiplying his time. He took this risk because he believed it would lead to an improved future.

For two million years, this homo roamed around Africa without significantly improving their condition. There were no real ways to make progress, when all your possessions and technologies had to be carried with you. It is debated whether we settled down because we learned how to domesticate plants or if we settled down because we learned how to produce low-alcohol beer. Perhaps both pieces of knowledge allowed us to make a quantum leap: for the first time in history, we could have a surplus of food and drink that were safe to consume thanks to yeast.

Imagine if you are a hunter-gatherer 10,000 years ago and you learn how to grow wheat, barley, or how to domesticate animals, so you don't have to hunt them in the wild. Imagine you work a plot of land for six months. Imagine you take care of your sheep every day. Imagine that on the day of the harvest, another hunter-gatherer comes and decides that all your production, all the sweat and tears of waking up at sunrise to work until sundown to take care of the plants for months on end, now belongs to him. He says, 'What is yours is also mine, so I take it, thank you very much.

What would your reaction be? Would you be pissed off? Of course you would, and for me, that is the birth of private property. Of capitalism and socialism. Of producers of wealth and thieves of previously accumulated wealth. All wealth has to be created; all wealth that has ever been, somebody had to work for it at a certain point in time.

The main difference lies in the kind of work done to obtain it. Was it earned through work, or was it acquired through theft? With the birth of wealth came the thieves - people who don't believe in private property. At its fundamental level, a thief doesn't believe in private property; that's why they can take what was originally yours.

Ever since then, the nature of our reality has not changed. The world still has people producing wealth, and it still has people who don't believe in private property and thus justify taking away your wealth. That is why, ever since the beginning of these times, wealth producers have had to protect themselves against pillagers. When they are stealing your property, you suddenly develop a sense of 'I have to defend myself, I have to protect it, and I have to behave in a way so as to minimize the risk of this happening.' This is one of the reasons why privacy is important. If you are able to secretly stash your wealth away from thieves, you increase your chances of being able to store your wealth for the future.

This development of commerce also brought about the need for money. It was the first time in history that we could accumulate a surplus, be it grains, animals, or whatever. Specialization and the division of labor were born. You could develop skills in one area of knowledge and further improve your productivity, to have an ever-growing surplus. If other people also have a surplus, it is the moment when we can start trading among ourselves, my surplus for your surplus. Some say that the first form of commerce was barter, trading what I have for what you have. Others say that this was very inconvenient, and we elaborated a way to keep track of debts in our heads. I gave you this in the past; therefore, you should give me this now. Either way, both systems present many problems.

With barter, it's very difficult to have a coincidence of wants. If you have apples and I have a horse, how many apples is a horse worth? Can I keep so many apples? Will they rot away? Can I give you a piece of the horse? Of course not, if I give you the leg of the horse, I won't have a living horse any more.

How do we agree on an exchange rate between apples and horses? We would have to bargain from the very beginning with no reference point. People's valuations are all different and subjective. You might be in dire need of a horse today, but perhaps tomorrow you do not value the horse as much, and I have no precise way of knowing how much you value it.

If we conduct a trade, that's when I can infer that if you traded your 5000 apples for my horse, you value the horse at more than 5000 apples. Otherwise, you would not have made the deal. If the horse is worth 3000 apples to you and I value it at 5000, no voluntary exchange will occur.

Therefore, money arises. People naturally select the best goods in the economy to be used as intermediary goods; that is, goods you obtain in order to exchange for other goods in the future. These are usually the most salable goods, which means goods that are the easiest to sell, goods where you lose the least amount of possible value when selling them.

This is the reason why we don't use houses as money. If I presented myself to do a trade with someone and offered my house, he might like it, he might not. It's in the best interest of the other party to seem disinterested in it. If I wanted to sell my house tomorrow, most likely I would have to sell for a very large discount compared to if I could wait for six months to a year to sell it. Also, every house is different; each has a subjective value to each person appraising it.

For all these reasons, humans selected goods with these characteristics as money:

Salability: Goods that, when sold, carry zero or very little discount and are extremely easy to sell, being in high demand.

Portability: Goods that can carry a lot of value in a small space.

Divisibility: Goods that can be divided for change.

Fungibility: Goods that are so similar to one another as to become indistinguishable in value when you have two units of the same good.

Scarcity and proof of work: Goods that are not free and not abundant in the market. If they were abundant, they would lose their value. If you could obtain them for free or falsify them, they would also eventually lose their value.

Only a few goods in nature present this characteristics and that is why societies mostly chose precious metals like gold and silver after having tried seashells, salt, glass beads, cacao beans, cattle, etc.

The market mechanism naturally selected the best goods to be used as money. The market did not need a central coordinator or planner to choose gold; it arose from competition against all other goods that were left in inferior positions to be used as money.

Why should you care about the quality of the money?, you may ask:
Because your choice of money will directly impact your life, your future, and the wellbeing of your loved ones.

Remember that ever since the beginning of times, there have been socialists, thieves of money, thieves of your property, and thieves of your time—your life.

That is why they will devise ways to lower the quality of money, to have control over it, up until what we have today: a group of people who literally have a money printer. What would you do and how would you behave if you had a money printer? What if you didn't have to work for money, aside from all the work that got you to the point of being in control of the money printer?

How powerful would you be if you could decide to whom you give that newly created money? How powerful would you be if you could do it without the majority of the population noticing?

What if this mechanism of free money creation allowed you to steal from people's lives, from people's time, hard work, at a distance, without them ever noticing it, and even positioning yourself as the saviour that is here to help.

It doesn't matter how much you work. If there are people in control of the money printer, they will most likely use it and steal your time by producing inflation. The word inflation comes from the Latin word 'Inflare', which means to pump something up, to blow air into a balloon, to blow money into the money supply.

If the rate of inflation surpasses the rate of economic growth, it doesn't matter how much you work; if you save in this currency, all your work will eventually go to zero.

That is fiat money: *'**Money created to be able to steal from you at a distance, without you noticing who did it***'.

In my country, Argentina, this year's rate of inflation will exceed 100%, meaning that if you worked for 40 years and saved in the currency that Argentine politicians tell you to save in, your life's work will go from 40 years to just under 20 years. Twenty years of your life's work, gone in just one year.

Next year it will go down again, to as if you only worked for 10 years. Then 5, then two and a half, and so forth, as it gets closer to zero and your life savings are gone, taken by 'the system', the issuers, the central banks.

Fiat money becomes, then, a way to enslave you—a mechanism to steal your life energy from a distance.

The fiat government, the fiat schools and universities, and the fiat media will tell you it's all because of greedy businessmen. Just as Ayn Rand* anticipated in her extraordinary novels, *beware the day when businessmen decide to take their capital and knowledge elsewhere, where they are treated best.*

This largely explains the wealth disparity among nations. Countries that respect property rights, have low taxes, and are easy to do business in, attract capital. The capital is used to boost production, and wages rise.

It's amazing how some projections put Singapore with a GDP per capita of 240,000 USD for the year 2040, whereas most likely countries like my own, if they don't change their policies, will be stuck in the 10,000 USD range. From the point of view of an individual worker, one month of work in Singapore will equate to two years of work in Argentina, expressed in dollar terms. Here is where it's easy to see how your time is valued differently, when there is more capital around you to multiply your work and creative capacities.

*Ayn Rand was a Russian-American writer and philosopher known for her novels advocating individualism, rational self-interest, and laissez-faire capitalism. Her best-known works include "The Fountainhead" and "Atlas Shrugged. See Apendix.

3.2 GOVERNMENT FINANCING

Governments are not supernatural entities; they are groups of individuals sharing the same story of control and monopoly of violence among the rest of individuals. Governments have running costs and sources of income, just like you and me. Governments are born or created, they can go broke, be conquered, or destroyed. This has happened all throughout history, innumerable times. It is good to realize that most governments are not the biggest wealth producers in society; the private sector is. All the wealth you see around you, every invention, the house you are living in, the clothes you are wearing, the paper or screen where you are reading this—somebody made it, somebody invented it. It came first from the mind of someone who thought to himself: 'Yes, I can do it. I will take the risk. I will forego immediate gratification and put the proof of work'. Most likely, that person did it for their own profit, for their own benefit.

Quoting Adam Smith:

"It is not from the benevolence of the butcher, the brewer, or the baker that we expect our dinner, but from their regard to their own self-interest. We address ourselves not to their humanity but to their self-love, and never talk to them of our own necessities, but of their advantages"

Wealth needs to be created, everything you see around you wasn't there, it's all artificial, man-made. If we didn't have wealth creation we would be in survival mode, living naked in the jungle or in caves just as we did for millions of years. If we believe that the wealth we have is not enough, that there is poverty in the world, then more wealth can be created, all it requires is work, time and the best decision making.

Since governments are not the biggest wealth producers at all, they become wealth takers in order to pay for government expenses. The mechanisms a government has are:

Taxation

Money printing

Debt

Confiscations

Selling of government assets

Taxation involves taking a cut from someone's work and property. Just as feudal lords and slave owners did in the past, only a part of what you make is considered yours by the government. They take it through the threat of force or by confiscation. If a government takes over 50% of your life's work, are you 50% slave, 50% free? What if it takes 80% of your work? What we know for sure is that if it took 100% of your life's work, you are a complete slave.

Money printing is theft. It is a surreptitious way to tax people without them noticing the cause of the effect: the generalized rise in prices. It is all done without resorting to legislating the amount of value extraction in Parliament, as most governments would have to do with new or higher taxes. A government can continue to siphon off all the value in the economy up until the latest consequences when money dies. You can see examples of this in the last decade by observing what Venezuela or Zimbabwe have done. An average wage in Venezuela reached the equivalent of 15 USD per month! Imagine, for a second, earning just half a dollar per day. That is what inflation can lead a nation to.

But a little inflation is good, right? That's like saying a little cancer is good, or a little theft, or a little impoverishment of the lower classes.

Today's public debt is essentially future taxes and printing future money. It is mortgaging future generations, imposing on them a burden they have neither voted for nor decided upon, thus basically enslaving them.

3.3 PATRIARCHY AND MONARCHY

Let's go back to the story of the first people who settled down and started to work on a piece of land. You had to defend your land against thieves, rapists, assassins, and usurpers. You had to defend yourself against con men and fraudsters as well.

You had to run your business efficiently, bringing products to market that people were willing to pay you for more than they cost to produce, therefore selling them at a higher price than what you value your produce. In a voluntary transaction, both parties win; both parties value the goods they are getting as being more valuable than what they give up in exchange. Otherwise, they wouldn't carry out the exchange. Both expect to be better off after the exchange.

Suppose your neighbors were also working on their own land but weren't as savvy in defending it or in producing the products that people wanted at the price they were willing to afford. Eventually, that neighbor would start eating away his capital, and at a certain point, he would decide to sell his land. In this example, you have such a huge surplus accumulated that you decide to buy his land because you see a business opportunity to produce more.

You take him on as your employee; now he won't have to worry about making predictions about future prices, costs, changes in demand, attacks from thieves, etc. He will just have a steady pay each month. You expand and multiply. You literally multiply. Your family grows as you are able to feed more children; all the family works on the land.

If we continue with this example of this successful family going forward, we can reach a point when the accumulated wealth allows to pay for security, for the building of walls, etc. You become the king of the land, the *sheik*, the royal family. The citadel owner. People in less developed positions come to ask for work from you. They are also willing to live inside the protection of your fortress for a price, a rent/tax you can charge them. It's a win-win for both.

Families that were able to accumulate capital through generations are the families that arose as owners of the land. It's not an easy task to accomplish; you have to put your effort into building the family name, the brand, and inculcating values and virtues that will preserve and grow capital through generations.

Of course, there were kings who did not only get rich through voluntary exchange. Let's call this the socialist king: kings whose way of acquiring wealth was through rampage, looting, and stealing. They declared war on another king's land and raised taxes on their population to extract the most value possible from them, literally milking their life's energy until the economy collapses.

Hard times create good men

Good men create good times

Good times create weak men

Weak men create hard times

All that the capitalist and peaceful king could do in such an attack against his kingdom, his patriarchy, was to defend himself at his expense. Some were successful, some were not, and they got pillaged away. My main point here is to go back to the basic principle: Ever since we started producing wealth, the wealth producers have been attacked by the non-believers in the private property principle. Capitalists can only defend against socialists and provide them with better products and services. Socialists can only offer theft, murder and consumption of capital.

3.4 WHY THE WORLD IS ANARCHIC

The *anarcho-capitalists** dream of a future world where everything is private, and you move from private property to private property, each with different rules and ways of owning the land. Examples of this could be a super-capitalist company like Apple running 'Apple country,' where everything is aesthetic, easy to use, and expensive. Another country might choose to be a socialist commune that doesn't use money. The key point the anarcho-capitalist wants to make here is that you are free to choose and that you would be able to vote with your feet. This system works as long as you are allowed to move around.

My take on the subject is that we are already living in that world. The world has always been anarchic. All the lands have an owner, and that owner is whoever is able to secure the safety and control of the land. You think you own land? You are actually renting your land. Most countries have taxes on property, whether it is land or houses. That means if a country is charging you two percent a year in property taxes, you don't fully own the land; you're renting it from the government, the real owner of the land. It equates to having to buy a similar property every 50 years. If you don't pay this tax, you lose your house or land; it wasn't yours.

*Anarcho-capitalists advocate for a stateless society where private property rights and free markets are the primary mechanisms for organizing society and resolving disputes.

3.5 ONE WORLD GOVERNMENT

There is no one-world government. Besides the intention of a group to institute a one-world government—a force pushing towards centralization and the enslavement of mankind by eliminating choice or alternatives—there is a force acting in the opposite direction towards decentralization. Bitcoin propels the world towards decentralization of power by making it harder for thieves to steal, and by making it more difficult to tax, as was the case before the widespread use of computers.

This consequence of making it more difficult to know who owns what or not will not disable governments from collecting taxes. Just as in the past, before computers, governments taxed on the size of your land, how wide the building was or how many windows it had.

3.6 THE CURRENT REAL OWNERS

Now that monarchy has lost it's flair and we live in fiat world, the true owners of the land are those who control the money supply. You can conceptualize a country's currency as a share in the national economy, akin to a company's stock, where a select few can arbitrarily issue new shares at their discretion, at no cost, and allocate them to those they consider most suitable. Often, this includes their allies in the media, companies colluding with politicians or owned by politicians, universities, the public sector, and the impoverished few who receive funds with the expectation of securing their vote. Some nations devalue their currencies to such an extent that they become stagnant economies, where genuine value is eroded day by day and economic calculation becomes impractical.

Therefore the current real owners are the ones in control of the printing press, or nowadays, the keyboard: The Central Bankers.

What bigger power than the power to create money at will and decide what to use it for. What bigger power than to not having to work for it and make others do the work for you.

3.7 FIAT IS THEFT

Fiat is a Latin term that means 'by decree' or 'by imposition of a ruler'. It's not something that was voluntarily chosen by people and markets, but rather imposed upon them under threat of force.

Force and guns are what you resort to when you can't seduce, convince, or offer a better product or service that people would voluntarily choose. Fiat currencies have inherited their value from previous gold-backed currencies and have become mechanisms for extracting value. Just as different iterations of the Argentine peso have lost over 99.99999% of their purchasing power, the dollar has lost 99% of its purchasing power.

3.8 NOMINAL VS REAL

Inflation distorts economic calculations, creating an illusion of profit when, in reality, one is losing money in real terms. Consider the following examples:

John received a 5% raise and felt pleased. However, with inflation at 10%, his salary effectively decreased by around 5%. He should have been dismayed.

Peter experienced a 2% wage cut and felt disheartened. Yet, with deflation at 5%, he actually received a pay increase of about 3%. He should have been elated.

Both John and Peter succumbed to *nominality*.

It's crucial to assess things in *real* terms rather than *nominal* terms. For instance, if the real estate market has been appreciating at 15% per year, is your 7% dividend yield a profit or a loss? Consider how many pounds or kilos of meat you can buy now compared to before, or how many gallons or liters of gas you can purchase with your salary. Could fiat economists claim that 'we are growing' when, in reality, we are losing capital?

3.9 THE FIAT NATURE OF WAR

Fiat *is a a tool of war.*

Its purpose is to finance them and to continue and grow the scale of war until all the economic value of a society is consumed through the inflation tax.

It is a tool of war, primarily used to finance conflicts and to sustain and expand them until the economic value of a society is consumed through the inflation tax. The ability to print money enables governments to fund wars without immediate tax increases, which might be unpopular among the public.

This can lead to significant inflation, effectively acting as a hidden tax on the population as the value of money decreases. The erosion of purchasing power impacts every citizen, as prices for goods and services rise due to the increased money supply chasing the same amount of goods.

Before the advent of central banks and fiat currency, wars were financed in different ways:

1. Direct Taxation: Governments would increase taxes to raise the necessary funds for war. This often led to public discontent and could limit the duration and scale of conflicts due to the finite tax base.

2. Borrowing: Monarchies and governments borrowed money from wealthy individuals, bankers, merchants, and other nations. This debt had to be repaid, usually with interest, placing a long-term burden on the economy.

3. Debasement of Coinage: Rulers often debased their coinage, reducing the precious metal content in coins to create more money. This was an early form of inflation and had similar effects on the economy, though it was generally less efficient than modern fiat systems.

4. Spoils and Looting: Victorious armies would loot defeated territories to finance their campaigns. This was a direct transfer of wealth and resources from one region to another.

5. Trade and Alliances: Some nations relied on trade or formed alliances with other countries to secure financial and military support. This could involve complex negotiations and commitments that might influence the course and outcome of conflicts.

The shift to fiat currency and central banking has fundamentally changed how wars are financed and sustained. This is why the 20th century saw two World Wars with millions of deaths. While it allows for rapid mobilization of resources and extended conflicts, it also leads to significant economic consequences for the populace. Inflation erodes savings, distorts economic signals, and can lead to long-term instability if not managed properly.

Understanding the historical context of war financing highlights the profound impact of monetary policy on global conflicts and the importance of maintaining a stable and transparent financial system to mitigate the adverse effects of war on society.

3.10 INFLATION IS THE WORST CRIME AGAINST HUMANITY AND CIVILIZATION

Inflation is *the silent tax.* I mention it as silent because few if any governments mention it considering what it does: It serves as a mechanism for redistributing wealth from the poor to the rich, facilitated by the money printing press.

When central banks increase the money supply by printing more currency, it leads to a general rise in prices for goods and services.

This inflation disproportionately affects lower-income individuals who rely on fixed incomes or savings denominated in the devalued currency.

Meanwhile, those with assets such as stocks, real estate, or businesses often see the value of their holdings rise in tandem with inflation or even outpace it, thereby preserving or increasing their wealth.

In essence, inflation *erodes the purchasing power of the poor while potentially enriching the wealthy,* exacerbating income disparity in society.

Inflation is life taking. Bitcoin is life giving.

3.11 THIEVES ARE SOCIALISTS, SOCIALISTS ARE THIEVES

Ever since we settled down and started working on agriculture, we can say that capitalists and socialists were born. Meet John, the capitalist, who would choose a territory to work on for six months in order to have a harvest. Work plus time equals output. Potential profit. He has a low time preference. Imagine if, on the day of the harvest, the thief or socialist presents himself and says: '*I am Paul, I am here to collect the harvest, I am going to take it all.*' Most likely, if you are the person who has worked for six months in the field, you will say: '*No way, this is mine.*'

This is where private property was born—when someone declared, 'This is mine.' That's also when socialism emerged; it's when someone claimed, 'What is yours is mine as well.' To be a socialist, to be a thief, you have to refuse to acknowledge the other person's right to their property. This is how a thief justifies taking another person's property. They don't believe in private property; if they did, they wouldn't touch someone else's property or desire it.

Every socialist is an undercover thief. A socialist doesn't want to convince you to voluntarily give your property to him; he doesn't negotiate for something you willingly choose to exchange. To establish socialism, he must take it against your will, resorting to theft, violence, or threats.

If he used voluntary means he would be in the realm of capitalism, not in the realm of socialism. Socialism is justified theft in the minds of those conducting it. Ever since the first John, life has been a opposition of capitalism vs socialism. Wealth producers against wealth takers. Wealth creation versus wealth leeching. Between individuals who believe in private property and those who don't.

Bitcoin is a tool of capitalism; it's the *epitome* of private property.

3.12 THE REAL REASON POLITICIANS PUSH TO REGULATE THE ECONOMY

They are playing with us, extracting our economic value. When you regulate the economy, you have the opportunity to grant privileges, preferences, to sell your positions, to be pressurized.. You gain insider information on what is going to happen because you change the rules of the game; you set the rules of the game. With that privileged information, you can leverage your positions and make orders of magnitude greater returns than if you were simply competing in an unregulated, free-market economy.

In a free market, I have to compete by providing the best service, the best product, the best prices, the shortest times, and the greatest customer satisfaction. I have to make assumptions about what the future preferences of consumers are going to be. I might fail in my assessments and go bankrupt or lose investors' money."

3.13 THE REAL REASON CENTRAL BANKS EXIST

Central Banking is a scam orchestrated by banks and governments. It's a relatively recent method of deceiving people, with an average lifespan of only a hundred years, depending on the country. The reason for its existence is to prevent banks and governments from going bankrupt, always at the expense of the population. It's a mechanism for shifting all the bad decisions and risks onto the average worker, who pays for the mistakes through the hidden tax of inflation.

There's a moral hazard at play here. When banks profit, they keep the profit, but when losses occur, new money can be created to bail out the banks. Similarly, if politicians overspend and governments run deficits, new money can cover the difference. Before central banks, if a bank made bad decisions, there might not have been anyone able to save it, and the bank would go bankrupt. The same applied to governments and monarchies. There was a benefit in making correct decisions and a punishment for bad ones.

Central Banks represent a union or marriage, if you like, between banks and governments, as they have devised a means to safeguard themselves by legalizing counterfeiting exclusively for their benefit, never for the people. Countries like Argentina serve as prime examples of how central banks evolve into soul-draining mechanisms, extracting 99.9999999% of the value from their currencies. Even the least extracting central banks, such as the US Federal Reserve, have depleted 99% of the value from the dollar. Consider this: if you required one hundred dollars in 1910 to make a purchase, today you'd need ten thousand dollars for the same purchase. Money is fundamentally broken in every country, and central banks are to blame.

Money printing also grants discretionary power. Those in control of the money printer can decide at will which banks they let fail and which banks they save, just as a Roman emperor would give the thumbs up or the thumbs down on who was going to live. Having the money printer is a great temptation. Even in the crypto world, everybody (except bitcoiners) wants to have the ability to print money at will and to have the discretion to decide to whom that money is allocated. Central Banks are a mechanism to steal from the poor. It is a wealth redistribution mechanism from the poor to the rich, who are at the top controlling the banks and the government.

The discretionary nature of the control on interest rates enables corrupt politicians and bankers to profit immensely from the decisions that they make. They can create booms and busts at will. Imagine what you could do if you knew which policy you were going to implement.

It is naive to assume that all central bankers in all countries are angels who will not inform their 'friends', 'Hey, we are going to raise interest rates tomorrow', or 'Hey, we are going to devalue the currency tomorrow'.

We need to end central banking now.

Fortunately, *we can just opt out of central banking with Bitcoin*.

3.14 EVERY GOVERNMENT LAW HAS THE POINT OF A GUN BEHIND IT

There are no government laws without the threat of physical violence to support them. A law states: whoever breaks this law will be punished accordingly. Even something as banal as forbidding people to smoke inside a restaurant is enforced by force. Imagine trying to defy such a simple regulation. You are the restaurant owner and you believe people should be allowed to smoke inside your establishment. You name it 'The Smokey Restaurant'. Your clients also wish to smoke, so you permit it on your premises.

Then one day, a municipal inspector visits and informs you: 'Smoking is forbidden inside restaurants, and you're breaking the law.' Your response: 'Here, we are smokers and will continue to smoke.' Shortly after, the inspector summons the nearest policeman, who reiterates the same message. You and your customers persist in smoking, asserting your freedom to do so within your private

113

property, Smokey Restaurant. The policeman then requests, 'Please come with me to the police department.' You refuse, stating firmly, 'No, I'm not going anywhere.' The policeman calls for backup, and soon five policemen arrive, attempting to restrain you by the arm. Believing they lack the right to touch you, you attempt to free yourself from their grasp.

Soon, you'll realize you are not supposed, in their view, to defend yourself. They are allowed to touch you, to search your body, thus allowed to rape you, to hit you with a stick, to kidnap you in their car, and to enslave you in a cell. Of course, you may say: why be so extremist? Somebody has to do it! The point I'm trying to make is that every law, as banal as forbidding smoking inside private property, has to end in the death of the lawbreaker if the lawbreaker believes he is in his right and defends himself.

What often happens within many countries is that the law is primarily enforced to those who are easy to target. Police and regulators *'hunt within a Zoo'*, a defined and controlled scope. Those who don't abide by the law and become 'difficult', catch the eye of the regulator, diverting attention elsewhere.

This approach relies on the use of power and authority to ensure compliance with laws and regulations, often leaving individuals with little room for voluntary decision-making. In such a system, the government exercises control through various means, including law enforcement, regulations, and the threat of punitive actions. This method aims to maintain order and stability, but it can also lead to a society where fear and compulsion overshadow personal freedom and autonomy. The inherent reliance on force raises questions about the balance between security and liberty, and whether a more consensual approach could achieve the same goals without undermining individual rights.

This is a superior approach: a society founded on voluntary, consensual interactions and transactions, devoid of coercion or exploitation. It entails organizing society in a manner where all involved parties actively choose to participate. This is the essence of what Bitcoin advocates.

3.15 A FREE AND OPEN SOCIETY

Only the private sector can offer voluntary interactions. That's why bitcoiners are builders. If we want to create a world with less consensual interactions (less rape and theft), we have to develop products and services that encourage people to choose the voluntary sector—capitalist enterprise—over the government's option enforced by law and police. In the 'Bitcoin Future' section, we'll discuss how Bitcoin will also lead to governments more aligned with freedom and less reliant on force.

3.16 WHAT ECONOMICS IS - OUR FINITE TIME ON EARTH

In history, there was a breaking point when the homo animal, previously living life like any other animal, sought to improve his conditions. We discovered fire around a million to 800,000 years ago, invented language only 50,000 years ago, and learned to practice agriculture and settle down, ceasing our nomadic wanderings 12 to 8 thousand years ago. This progression has led us along the path of improving our condition from mere survival to Bitcoin and beyond. We developed rational thinking, abstract concepts, mathematics, theories, and religions. We discovered money, the division of labour, the concept of justice, weapons, and private property. The concept of time became integral to our existence. We became *'homo economicus'*.

Homo economicus is the creature that has resolved to enhance its condition. We have a finite time in this life; this is our ultimate scarcity, the resource that cannot be counterfeited. We can only project our consciousness forward onto our children, onto the next generations. Given your finite time on Earth, what will your experience be? One of mere survival, or will you strive for the best possible experience? What will be the best use of your ultimate currency, your seconds of life? Do you choose sacrifice in the sense of selecting the worst option, or do you opt for what you believe will be best for you and those you care about? After this choice comes action; action requires work.

Every living organism is working in order to live. Each living organism consumes inputs to produce outputs. Between input and output, there must be a surplus, a profit. The day the cell starts consuming more than it produces is the day that organism begins to die. Life is work. The absence of work is death. Life is continuous work, and that is a good thing; life is a force that fights against nothingness and chooses to be something, for a while.

There is a direct lineage connecting you to the first living organism. The initial living organism left a part of itself to develop into the next living organism. Subsequently, that organism passed on a portion of its code and atoms to the next one, and so forth—the DNA coding process. You are composed of equal parts of your father and mother, literally made from them—a continuation of their essence, extending back through all preceding generations to the emergence of life billions of years ago.

Economizing is an attempt to use our finite resources in the way we deem best. We make decisions based on what we know at the time; we cannot predict the future, only estimate it. Economizing involves achieving the best possible outcome using the fewest resources available. It is about maximizing profit, creating wealth, and sustaining life.

You come from being an animal just surviving in the jungle, desert, or savannah. Now, look around you. Everything you see—the house you're in, the paper or screen where you're reading this, Bitcoin, the language you're using—it's all artificial, man-made. Someone invented it, someone produced it, someone wanted to live by providing it.

Wealth must be created, and it originates solely from the human mind and human action. The only constraint on human wealth and progress is the time we dedicate to work. You have the choice to leverage time in your favour: learning from the past, acting in the present, and speculating on the future. This involves developing a time preference: will you focus solely on today, or will you also consider your well-being for tomorrow? Are you prepared to invest in your future?

One of the best examples Austrian economists like to use is the tale of a fisherman. He can only catch two fish a day with his bare hands, which is what he needs to sustain his life. In order to build a spear that he speculates will enable him to catch four fish a day, he has to quit catching fish for two days. He has to invest his time and resources, foregoing consumption for a future benefit, a possible future profit and outcome. Perhaps he is wrong, and the spear is no good. Perhaps he is wrong, and catches six fish a day instead of four. He fasts for two days, builds a spear, and he was correct; he can now catch four fish a day. He now has a profit; he can save two extra fish a day. He can pay another man two fish a day for a month to give him a net to catch fish. This exchange was voluntary and entailed trust. But now the fisherman can catch ten fish a day.

If he had been lazy or concerned about 'sacrificing' two days without consumption, fasting, he would never have embarked on the path of improving his condition by building the first spear.

His pursuit of self-interest led him down the path of acquiring a spear, and eventually, a fishing net. Now, with an extra eight fish per day, he can introduce this newfound abundance into the market. The market thrives on voluntary interactions; one person may trade coconuts for fish, while another might offer salt or olive oil. Each participant engages in trade because they believe they will benefit from the exchange. They may be mistaken, but it's their error to make —a valuable learning experience. Ultimately, trade benefits all involved parties. A free-market economy operates on consent; resorting to coercion or threats to facilitate trade ventures into criminal territory.

The fisherman accumulated capital by temporarily foregoing consumption and investing in spear technology and fishnet technology. As a result, he now catches eight fish a day, compared to his previous output of one fish every four hours of work, now increased to five fish every four hours. This represents economic progress, as it involves the multiplication of time by freeing up more time.

Imagine for a moment if you had to be self-sufficient in the sense that you couldn't engage in economic trade with other human beings. You would have to learn to make your own clothes, hunt your own animals, and build your own home; you'd essentially be living like Tarzan in the jungle. No hospitals, no medicines, no electricity, no iPhones, no Bitcoin. To those who advocate for returning to self-sufficiency, I say, there is nothing stopping you from going to the jungle and living like Tarzan. Civilization is optional, but it requires work.

3.17 AUSTRIAN ECONOMICS

Austrian economics is the study of human action. It differs from the economics taught in mainstream universities and colleges of fiat culture. It does not presuppose that all actors act rationally or possess perfect information. Instead, it provides a humane understanding of economics, acknowledging that we are flawed individuals who act based on what we believe is best, recognizing our limited knowledge and propensity for mistakes. Austrian economics acknowledges that knowledge is decentralized and constantly evolving. It advocates for organizing society and the economy through voluntary interactions, emphasizing that whenever a central planner sets the course of the economy with 'good intentions,' they pave the way to hell.

3.18 A MARKET PRICE AS A HASH OF ALL HUMAN KNOWLEDGE AND PREFERENCES

In a previous section, we explored the concept of a hash function, which generates a unique identifying number from a finite pool of options based on a given set of information.

In a free economy, the market price reflects the sum of all individual knowledge and preferences condensed into a single figure. This price is not static; preferences and knowledge are constantly changing, so fluctuations in prices are to be expected. Calculating a market price is a complex process that no aspiring central planner can accomplish, as they cannot access the minds and preferences of each participating individual. Instead, they may resort to using force to impose an artificial price they deem optimal, which may diverge from the market price.

3.19   THE ECONOMY IS FRACTAL

The economy behaves as fractal, with similar patterns and structures appearing at multiple scales within the economic system, reflecting a self-similar nature. This helps in understanding the inherent complexity and interconnectedness of economic activities. Here are several reasons and examples illustrating why the economy is fractal:

Market Structures and Patterns: Financial markets exhibit fractal patterns in price movements and trading volumes. For instance, the fluctuations in stock prices over short periods often resemble the fluctuations observed over longer periods. This self-similarity is a hallmark of fractal systems, suggesting that the mechanisms driving market behavior are consistent across different time scales.

Supply Chains: The structure of supply chains can also be viewed as fractal. A local business might source materials from various suppliers, each of which has its own network of suppliers. This nested, hierarchical structure can be observed at multiple levels, from small businesses to multinational corporations, demonstrating a repeating pattern of dependency and interaction.

Economic Cycles: Business cycles (booms and busts) are another example of fractal behavior. Small economic shocks can ripple through the economy, leading to larger cycles of expansion and contraction. Similarly, the overall economy's long-term growth patterns may exhibit similar cycles on a grander scale, reflecting the fractal nature of economic dynamics.

Understanding the economy as fractal provides valuable insights into its resilience and vulnerability. It highlights the importance of local actions and policies, recognizing that changes at one level can influence the entire system. This also emphasizes the need for holistic solutions, considering the interconnectedness and cascading effects within the economy.

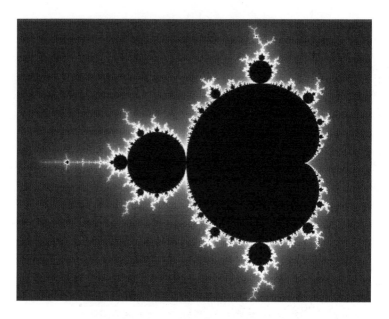

'The Mandelbröt set', a famous fractal that can only be drawn by computers. *Wikipedia image*

3.20 THE MARKET MECHANISM AS A COMPUTING ENTITY

*"By preferring the support of domestic to that of foreign industry, he intends only his own security; and by directing that industry in such a manner as its produce may be of the greatest value, he intends only his own gain, and he is in this, as in many other cases, led by an **invisible hand** to promote an end which was no part of his intention."*

—Adam Smith

When we compare how our brains function, learning from past mistakes, making new ones, gathering thousands and millions of data points throughout our life to make the best decisions possible. When we see how the neural networks of the current AIs are modeled after our brains using statistical simulations, that AI's learn just by comparing lots of data points and 'guessing' the best possible solution, we can start to see the market as a supra entity that is working towards an outcome we cannot know of. Every voluntary economic interaction is a computation, a choice that is trying to benefit the two parties involved. It's a transformation from worst to better.

What will the output of this computation be? Does it ever stop? Is it the rise of AI? What will the AIs come up with once they interact with each other in the market? What comes after AI? Consuming all the energy possible to compute, to live, to forever expand consciousness until all matter is put to compute, to think? What if all matter is already computing and we cannot see it yet. Just as a dog cannot understand our rationality and just as there was a point in time in which we didn't have rationality, there could be a step above rationality that we cannot now comprehend. And a step beyond that. Can an ant understand you? We might never be able to understand AI.

Just as cells in your body are sending signals to other cells, with messenger proteins and hormones to regulate a 'equilibrium' so is the market constantly sending signals of what is being demanded, what is no longer needed, what is being preferred, what needs to be done next.

3.21 VAT AND INCOME TAX ARE VARIATIONS OF THE SAME THING

Countries like Argentina have a 21% Value Added Tax and a 35% Income Tax. The rationale behind this two 'different' taxes is that one is taxing 'the added value' and the other is taxing 'profits'.

Let's delve into income tax first: For corporations, it is calculated after deducting expenses from revenues. If your company makes $363,000 in revenue and has $121,000 in expenses, you pay

35% of the profit, which amounts to $242,000. The total income tax comes to $84,700. For individuals, it is calculated by subtracting income from a few allowed deductions.

VAT works in a similar fashion. Your expenses are $100,000 plus VAT, and you pay $121,000 for your purchases. Your sales are $300,000 plus VAT, and you collect $363,000 from your customers. The netting of VAT sales ($63,000) minus VAT purchases ($21,000) is what you have to pay to the government as VAT. So, subtracting $21,000 from $63,000, you owe $42,000 to the government.

Notice that even though the methods of calculation differ, the outcome is the same. What differs from one tax to the other is that in VAT, there are some expenses you cannot deduct, such as the payroll for your employees. Your employees likely do not provide you with a bill including VAT. While you might receive bills with VAT from lawyers or accountants, your main employees do not. In VAT, you cannot deduct expenses from other taxes, whereas in income tax, you can deduct what you have paid in other taxes.

My argument is that these two taxes are very similar and were separated into two because stating that we are taxing 56% of what you produce is unpopular.

If all taxes were dutifully paid, then 56% of the economy goes to the government since everything you see around you, every wealth there is profit, is added value. More than half of one's lifetime is spent navigating these two taxes alone, akin to modern-day enslavement.

3.22 CBDCs - CENTRAL BANKING ON STEROIDS

A new global threat is looming in the horizon: the rise of Central Bank Digital Currencies. Inspired by 'crypto' and the Chinese communist government, many of the world's central banks have started to tinker with the idea and project of launching their own digital version of the dollar, euro, etc.

Their aim is to have a society that is all under surveillance of the central bank where each member of the population has an app on his phone with a digital balance of money in the central banks ledger. This centralized control of all people's money lends itself to total domination. The state will know everything you do, where you do it, your preferences and your account will get manipulated at a distance.

Modern Monetary Theorists would love to tinker with the economy. Not enough spending? Let's make it so that if you don't use your digital, centrally controlled dollars, they expire, or they are reduced in value. Imagine what a corrupt government could do: freeze the account of dissidents or disable your ability to receive new funds.

With the 2030 Agenda in mind they could track the CO_2 of the products and services you buy and put limits on it. You made a transatlantic flight this year? No more flying for you. You ate meat? No more for you, here is cricket protein powder. CBDC's are every socialist and aspiring dictator's wet dream. All the lives of the population at your discretion.

3.23   CBDCs ARE PERONISM

In March 1946, Argentine military general Perón asked President Farrell to nationalize the Central Bank and appointed Miguel Miranda as its President of the Board. The presidents of the Banco de la Nación, Banco de Crédito Industrial Argentino, and Banco Hipotecario Nacional were part of the Central Bank's board.

A month later, a presidential decree resulted in what was called "the nationalization of bank deposits": the Central Bank would guarantee all bank deposits, set the interest rate to be paid to depositors, and compensate banks for those payments. Banks could not use the deposits to lend to their clients, but the Central Bank would discount past and future loans and other banking investments in amounts and conditions (purpose of the loans, interest rates, and terms) that would be pre-established for each individual bank. In practice, banks would act as mere executors of the Central Bank, which would become the sole institution capable of deciding the allocation of credit and its conditions.

4. Bitcoin Future

4.1 BITCOIN HAS DECLARED CHECKMATE TO FIAT

Eight days after the Genesis Block (Bitcoin's launch in January 3rd, 2009), Hal Finney, a pioneering computer scientist and cypherpunk, replied to Satoshi's announcement email of the release of Bitcoin with a few thoughts on how Bitcoin could appreciate over time. He wrote:

```
To: satoshi@vistomail.com
Cc: bitcoin-list@lists.sourceforge.net,
cryptography@metzdowd.com
Date: Sat, 10 Jan 2009 18:22:01 -0800 (PST)
From: hal@finney.org ("Hal Finney")

Satoshi Nakamoto writes:
> Announcing the first release of Bitcoin, a new
electronic cash
> system that uses a peer-to-peer network to prevent
double-spending.
> It's completely decentralized with no server or
central authority.
>
> See bitcoin.org for screenshots.
>
> Download link:
> http://downloads.sourceforge.net/bitcoin/
bitcoin-0.1.0.rar

Congratulations to Satoshi on this first alpha
release.  I am looking forward to trying it out.

> Total circulation will be 21,000,000 coins.  It'll
be distributed
> to network nodes when they make blocks, with the
amount cut in half
> every 4 years.
>
> first 4 years: 10,500,000 coins
> next 4 years: 5,250,000 coins
> next 4 years: 2,625,000 coins

> next 4 years: 1,312,500 coins
> etc...
```

It's interesting that the system can be configured to only allow a certain maximum number of coins ever to be generated. I guess the idea is that the amount of work needed to generate a new coin will become more difficult as time goes on.

One immediate problem with any new currency is how to value it. Even ignoring the practical problem that virtually no one will accept it at first, there is still a difficulty in coming up with a reasonable argument in favor of a particular non-zero value for the coins.

As an amusing thought experiment, imagine that Bitcoin is successful and becomes the dominant payment system in use throughout the world. Then the total value of the currency should be equal to the total value of all the wealth in the world. Current estimates of total worldwide household wealth that I have found range from $100 trillion to $300 trillion. With 20 million coins, that gives each coin a value of about $10 million.

So the possibility of generating coins today with a few cents of compute time may be quite a good bet, with a payoff of something like 100 million to 1! Even if the odds of Bitcoin succeeding to this degree are slim, are they really 100 million to one against? Something to think about...

Hal

It seems quite astounding to me that when Bitcoin was only seven days old and just a couple of men were on the network running the software, and the coin had zero value, there was already one user estimating that Bitcoin could be worth 10 million dollars one day. What a powerful vision. Yet Hal's price predictions were in real terms —that is, in the equivalent purchasing power of 2009 dollars. Therefore, we can do a new calculation thinking in nominal terms; that is, what would happen to fiat money during a hyperbitcoinization? Let's consider how the Bitcoin adoption process will unfold pricewise. Let's run some numbers and make some simplifications for the sake of understanding the process of Bitcoin's monetization.

SCENARIO A, 1% adoption

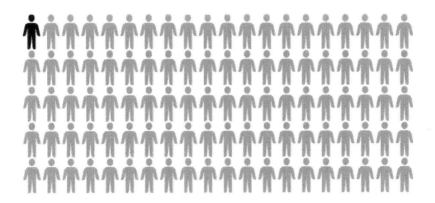

Let's start with SCENARIO A where Bitcoin is at $50,000 per Bitcoin and it has a market capitalization of around $1 Trillion. We are going to assume for the sake of this thought experiment that the world's total money market equates to 100 Trillion in dollar terms. Therefore Bitcoin would have around 1% of the money market and we can say that it has a 1% market penetration. Fiat money is 99% of the market.

SCENARIO B, 10% adoption

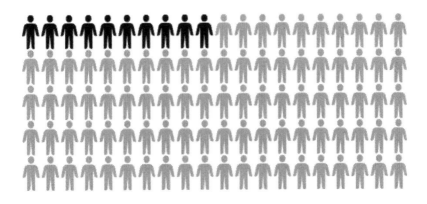

A few years go by, and one, two, or three bull and bear cycles later, Bitcoin reaches a 10% market adoption or a price similar to $500,000 per Bitcoin. This means that if the world were only comprised of 100 individuals, 9 persons would join the Bitcoin ship, and in order to do so, they have to spend their fiat money to acquire those Bitcoins. The fiat goes to the hands of the 90 people still remaining in the fiat world. These 90 people now own 100 pieces of fiat, effectively having 10% more fiat than before. This means that they will eventually experience a 10% inflation of fiat-denominated prices. The only way for this not to happen would be for governments to take this extra 10% out of circulation, deflating the fiat currency supply.

What do Bitcoiners experience when we go from 1% adoption to 10% adoption? Hyperdeflation. Just as Bitcoiners have experienced since the beginning of Bitcoin. If a cup of coffee was 10,000 sats or $5 at 1% adoption, then it would decrease to just 1,000 sats at 10% adoption. If we account for the 10% fiat inflation, the coffee's new price would be $5.50 or 1,100 sats.

SCENARIO C, 50% adoption

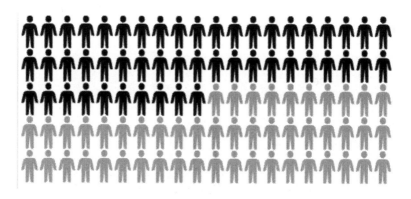

Bitcoin has reached half of the world money market. 50% market share. In this world of only 100 inhabitants it means that 50 individuals have gotten rid of their fiat and handed it over to the 50 individuals still remaining in fiat. People remaining in fiat now have double the money, resulting in a 100% inflation, a doubling of prices since they have twice the fiat.

The Bitcoiner experiences hyperdeflation of prices, with them decreasing to 1/5 of what they were before. The Bitcoin price would be $2,500,000 (in real terms or SCENARIO A dollars) per Bitcoin in this scenario. However, measured in devalued, 100% inflated SCENARIO C dollars, the price of a BTC is $5,000,000. The same cup of coffee is now 200 satoshis or $10.

SCENARIO D, 99% adoption

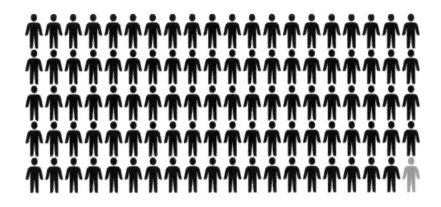

In this scenario, we're in a hyper-bitcoinized world where Bitcoin reaches 99% adoption. This means that 49 more individuals join the Bitcoin ship, disposing of their fiat, leaving only one individual with all the fiat for themselves. That lone individual will experience a 100X rise in fiat prices. Meanwhile, Bitcoiners just experience a halving of their prices. The latte moves to 100 sats, and in fiat terms, it hyperinflates to $500! Measured in SCENARIO A dollars, the Bitcoin price is just $5,000,000. However, since fiat currencies would be practically dead, hyperinflated away, Bitcoin's price measured in SCENARIO D dollars is $500,000,000!

As Bitcoin progresses the fiat money gets even more devalued, faster. Bitcoin gets monetized through deflation while fiat currency gets demonetized through hyperinflation. What will you choose?

The existence of Bitcoin is a checkmate to fiat. It's only a matter of time. When you have one currency hyperdeflating, hyperincreasing your purchasing power, and another currency hyperinflating, hyperdecreasing your purchasing power, the decision is a no-brainer. Gresham's Law kicks in, the economic law that states that the simultaneous presence of bad money and good money in the economy makes it so that people want to get rid of their bad money first and hoard or HODL their good money.

4.2 SCENARIO Z - BITCOIN TEACHING GOVERNMENTS TO BEHAVE LIKE BITCOIN

The alternative to the scenarios explained in the previous section is for governments to realize that people now have an alternative, a way to escape the corral they've been put into with fiat currencies. As Bitcoin adoption grows, governments must recognize the need to offer a competitive alternative. The only way to halt the inflation and hyperinflation of their fiat currencies is for governments to cease printing and actually remove currency from circulation.

That would mean that governments would need to have a surplus in their treasuries, some savings to the scenarios explained in the previous section is for governments to realize that people now have an alternative, a way to escape the corral they've been put into with fiat currencies.

That also requires governments to not have any more deficits but instead have a surplus, the only way to truly save. This would, at least, stabilize the prices of goods and services measured in fiat.

Do you think that governments that have continuously been in a deficit state, essentially being perpetually broke, governments that have been depending on stealthily extracting their population's wealth, will somehow change course and be willing to run their operations with a surplus, and also deflate the fiat currency supply?

If that happened then it would mean that Bitcoin changed the governments of the world.

This SCENARIO Z means that Bitcoin has taught governments and central banks to behave and to compete with a better form of money. Another variant of this scenario is central banks also deciding to acquire Bitcoin for their reserves, just as they do today with gold reserves. Bitcoiners will have won in this scenario as well, for Bitcoin will have introduced competition in the money market, improving the quality of fiat money.

But, as has happened innumerable times in the past, a gold standard is not as safe as having actual gold. Governments default on their promises precisely when people need their money the most, especially in recessions. A fiat currency backed by bitcoin is just as risky as a fiat backed by gold. Fortunately, with Bitcoin, it's possible to custody your own Bitcoin and not to rely on any third party. You can be Bitcoin sovereign if you get the know-how.

4.3 IN ORDER TO ARTIFICIALLY STABILIZE PRICES SOMEONE HAS TO STEAL THE PRODUCTIVITY GAIN

The only way to stabilize prices in a growing economy is to siphon the deflation out of the people. In an economy untouched by intervention, economic growth translates into cheaper prices. By hiding behind the mask of *'Deflation is bad'*, central bankers and politicians can justify printing money and stealing that deflation from you.

4.4 THE FIAT UNO

We've all heard stories of early Bitcoin transactions. Perhaps the most famous one is the offer made on the Bitcoin Talk Forum, where Lazlo paid 10,000 Bitcoin for two large Papa John's pizzas. As of this writing, those are the most expensive pizzas in history, as those 10,000 Bitcoin are now worth over 200 million dollars

In Argentina, we have the story of Luis Daniel, a gamer who began mining Bitcoin in his home early on and made his first used car purchase thanks to Bitcoin. Luis paid 77 BTC in exchange for $25,000 pesos in 2013, which was around 3000 USD at the time. He bought a 2005 Fiat Uno, a car designed in the 80s that was produced in Argentina until the early 2000s.

As of this writing, a Bitcoin is worth over 80 million pesos each in Argentina. So if Luis had kept his coins instead of selling them for $25,000 pesos, he would now have over six billion pesos in just eleven years! This showcases the power of Bitcoin in an inflationary country like Argentina. In US dollars, his $3,000 would now be worth over 5 million dollars. Interestingly, the price of a 2005 Fiat Uno is still hovering around $2,700 USD, indicating not the greatness of the Fiat car, but rather the inflation of the dollar, which is almost keeping pace with the depreciation of used cars.

2005 MODEL FIAT UNO

4.5 EMBRACE THE VOLATILITY, THERE IS NO WAY AROUND IT

I hear people say, *'Bitcoin will be money when it's no longer volatile.'* Mark Cuban, a famous American billionaire, once said, *'I will invest in Bitcoin when my grandmother uses bitcoin.'* They are missing the point.

Satoshi introduced a new form of money in 2009. Initially it was worth zero and it exhibited zero volatility. People were freely sending thousands of bitcoins around. Bitcoin websites, known as 'faucets,' offered 5 free bitcoins to whoever visited them. Then came the famous two pizzas on May 22, 2010, marking a historic moment celebrated each year as the Bitcoin Pizza Day around the world.

If your objective as a Bitcoiner is for Bitcoin to be used as a dominant currency or a dominant reserve asset, the Bitcoin economy has to reach the tens of trillions, if not the hundreds of trillions, of dollars. How do you grow something that, at one moment, was worth zero to climb in value into the tens or hundreds of trillions of dollars? In how many years? 20 years? 30? 50? 100? 200? Can you set a predefined rate of growth? How much would that predefined increase in value need to be? 50% per year for 50 years? 100% per year? Who would define it? Who would control it or be able to enforce it? Who would profit?

This same questions applies to any other attempt to compete with Bitcoin. I often hear some people say, 'No, they should make a new coin that is worth little, for the common man.' I reply with: *Who would enforce that only the little man uses it? How do you keep the value low?* Only a coin police could try to enforce such a thing, and fortunately, there is no Bitcoin police, nor is it possible to have such a thing.

What would happen to an economy *if you knew for a fact*, as if somebody could establish or decree it, that there is an asset that will appreciate at a defined rate of 100% per year, a doubling in value of your net worth every year, for years to come? Why work in something else? Why not put everything today, quit everything? Why wouldn't everybody do the same?

Fortunately, there is no way to have a predetermined rate of growth. Growth can only come in waves: bull markets followed by market crashes, followed by periods of range-bound movement or *lateralization*, where the price remains within a certain range for months, essentially going nowhere.

Bitcoin has been behaving exactly as it's naturally inclined to do. Its behavior has remained consistent throughout its history, and it will likely continue in this manner until it captures over half of the money market.

4.6 THE MOMENT WE CAN START PRICING IN SATOSHIS

In SCENARIO C, with 50% or more adoption, it becomes reasonable to price every good and service in Satoshis. Upon surpassing the 50% market share mark, the deflation of prices expressed in Satoshis slows down significantly, while the inflation of fiat prices accelerates considerably, leading to hyperinflation. Consequently, prices become much more stable when expressed in Satoshis than in any other currency. The incentives shift, making it easier to start pricing everything in Sats.

4.7 IT'S GOING UP FOREVER LAURA, FOREVER

Given the systemic nature of Bitcoin and fiat, the Bitcoin price never reaches its end goal because, as we saw in SCENARIO E, a 99% adoption would mean a $500 million nominal price. I don't expect governments to start behaving differently in the near future, meaning they will continue to debase their fiat currencies, adding 'more wood to the fire'.

If your assumptions are that humans continue to grow their economy, meaning that we don't stop in our quest to produce more with less, and also that we don't kill each other or get extinguished as a race, then BTC's purchasing power will forever and ever appreciate. Let that sink in for a moment.

4.8 INFINITE / 21M —> 0

Swedish Bitcoin advocate, author, and educator Knut Svanholm popularized the meme ∞/21M:

I here come to reformulate the meme because the total supply of Bitcoin tends to zero over time. Satoshi's coins are continually being lost and once they are lost they cannot be brought back to life.

It happens every day when people *lose their private keys*. Those coins sit in the Bitcoin blockchain for all of us to see, but we only observe coins that remain stationary. There is no way of knowing if they are lost forever or if they are retained because the owner is saving their coins for later use. We can only ascertain if a coin is 'alive' at the moment the owner of the private key signs a new transaction moving the coins.

When you have a forever-expanding economy divided by a finite and perpetually shrinking money supply with which to measure that economy, you get an infinite result. The infinite divided by an indefinitely shrinking finite number remains infinite.

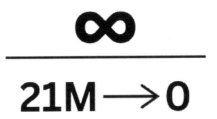

4.9 YOUR FINITE SHARE OF BTC BUYS YOU THE INFINITE THROUGH TIME

Whatever amount of Bitcoin you hold, you own a share of a forever shrinking finite total supply.

In a bitcoinized economy, two things will happen: on the one side, people will continue to lose their private keys, so bitcoins will continue to 'die' for the rest of time. This means that there will never be 21 million functional, 'alive' coins. When coins die, the real supply shrinks, making the remaining coins in circulation more scarce and valuable.

On the other side, the fact that Bitcoin has a finite supply turns the economy into a deflationary one. This means that when the economy grows, prices have to shrink.

When you take both factors into account, there are two forces working towards appreciating the value of your bitcoins. If your assumptions are that the global economy doesn't stop growing, we don't kill each other, and people continue to lose their coins, then what it means is that through time, your BTC will forever and ever continue to appreciate. That means that even though you have a finite amount, Bitcoin has bought you the infinite through time.

Just make sure *not to lose them*, and you'll be able to pass them on to the next generation.

4.10   A DONATION TO MANKIND

You can also choose to destroy your BTC or let them die with you and you will be shrinking the total supply, appreciating the remaining Bitcoin in circulation. It's the most effective, quick, tax free and proportional method to donate your capital, your life's work to the rest of the bitcoiner population. Michael Saylor, one of the biggest holders of Bitcoin in the world has hinted to this possibility for when he dies.

Satoshi himself could have done this as well. There are estimates that he mined approximately one million coins during the first two years of Bitcoin history, yet as we can see on the blockchain, he hasn't moved any of them. Those Bitcoin are currently worth in excess of 70 Billion dollars, so either Satoshi is still holding for a better time or he has decided to 'kill his coins' and take them out of circulation, only benefiting the rest of bitcoiners. If that is the case, he has not only created the best form of money for all mankind without asking anything in return but he has done the biggest donation ever.

4.11   THE ORANGE HOLE

In the current fiat world, people need to find ways to escape their national currencies. Whoever remains and saves in fiat loses all of their life's work eventually. That's why people turn to the real estate market, the stock market, and bond markets as their savings devices. We say these markets get 'monetized' or carry a 'monetary premium' because they experience demand that exceeds what would occur in a sane monetary world. In Argentina, we have the expression that the safest saving is in 'bricks'. So houses and lots are demanded in excess of what people would naturally do if the money were not corrupt. Thus, we can understand that in a bitcoinized world where your money continuously appreciates, many people will resort to just saving Bitcoin. The real estate, stock market, and bond market would get 'demonetized', and Bitcoin would have a gravitational pull that would suck in all existing value for the purpose of escaping fiat. Bitcoin becomes the orange hole, attracting value forevermore.

Thus, Bitcoin will make living in a home more affordable, as people realize that holding Bitcoin is much easier than holding homes and lots. As a result, home prices fall, and life becomes easier.

'If there is an escape, that escape will be used.'

Christine Lagarde, European Central Bank President

4.12 WINNERS AND LOSERS OF THE FUTURE ECONOMY

We have to thank God or 'the universe' for the diverse nature of reality. The idea behind Bitcoin cannot be stopped; it's out, and now it cannot be removed from our minds. The absolute digital scarcity Satoshi discovered will continue to attract value to it. At the same time, many countries will still behave as if we lived in a fiat-only world, debasing their currencies and impoverishing their populations.

As Christine Lagarde suggested, Bitcoin functions as that escape valve, a lifeboat for any capital trying to survive oppression, any capital seeking greener pastures. Just as we have today, there will continue to be Bitcoiner businessmen, Bitcoiner politicians, and even Bitcoin governments and central banks. We have already seen the example of a country adopting Bitcoin as legal tender. Many more will follow, countries that prefer to invest in a neutral asset, countries that want to ride the Bitcoin adoption upside.

We still have two to three orders of magnitude to go before we reach a Bitcoin standard. This means Bitcoin still has to grow by 100 times. A government or central bank investing a little today will take significant purchasing power into the future. Central banking betting on fiat will only see its reserves loose purchasing power.

4.13 THE BIGGEST THREAT TO BITCOIN

The greatest risk to Bitcoin is centralization. It is in the best interest of every Bitcoiner to keep it as it is today: the most decentralized monetary network and asset that has ever existed. Many private institutions and governments saving in Bitcoin will see it as in their best interest to keep the network decentralized, as all the investment loses value if one party can control the network. This is a new paradigm shift. For the first time, it is clear and evident to all participants that it is in everyone's interest to keep Bitcoin decentralized. Additionally, we have to bear in mind that Satoshi has initiated a hashing power race that cannot be stopped.

We will forever be adding hashing power to the network. This demand for hashing power will drive chip design and manufacturing technologies forward. These benefits will trickle down to other chips and technologies as well.

However, what if a company or government agency develops chip technology that is a leap forward and leaves other manufacturers at a disadvantage? Bitcoin chip design becomes a matter of national security in that scenario, and I don't envision competing governments enforcing the 20-year restrictions of patent laws.

They will likely break them in their self-interest of preservation. The same happens in an scenario where Quantum computers start to be deployed and are protected by laws and there is a monopoly on the technology. Whoever has this technology will have a hashing power advantage. That is why it's in Bitcoin's best interest for the deployment of new computing technologies to remain distributed and decentralized. It will be in the biggest BTC holder's interests to push chip manufacture speed and technology move forward as fast as possible.

Advances in chip manufacture will trickle down to other chips, meaning faster computing and more artificial intelligence to serve more economic growth.

4.14   BITCOIN IS ETHICAL INVESTING - WHY YOU SHOULDN'T SHITCOIN

If you visit CoinMarketCap.com you will see that there are in excess of a Million different cryptos listed. Shitcoins, whether they are other 'altcoins' or fiat government currencies, 99% of those listed represent an attempt by some group or individual to create value out of thin air, get rich quick without any proof of work involved, for near-zero cost. They are a fraud, preying on the less educated in economics and history, extracting value from 'the fools'. While the majority of them may experience a rise in price and produce profits at some point, someone else is losing, and the biggest profiteers are the individuals behind the curtain, running the show. They typically follow a pump-and-dump pattern, only to disappear later with the bag, sometimes claiming failure. The unethical behavior prevalent in the crypto world is a detriment to Bitcoin adoption.

This is why it's so important to learn to separate the wheat from the chaff, and learn that other crypto tokens have their risks involved as explained in the Proof of Stake section. In almost all crypto projects you are subordinate to the will of the founders. If the founders are honest the alt coin might do well. If the founders are secret scammers, then you are at their will and mercy. You will found out once the rug pull attack happens.

Bitcoin, on the other hand, is based on ethical standards grounded in reality, mathematics, and finitude, not theft. Only those who have worked for them are able to create Bitcoins. They cannot be faked out of thin air by the whim of a person or ruler. If you have the option to choose between supporting a moral, neutral system or more of the same fiat world, I hope you choose the former.

4.15   BITCOIN AND FEMINISM

Feminists claim there is a wage gap between men and women, of around 20 to 30% difference. Personally, I don't believe in that gap, as it would be highly profitable to hire all women if they were willing to do the same work for 30% less pay. Women could benefit from this situation as well by starting their own businesses and beating other businesses in the market.

Let's talk about the real gap. Men hold almost all the Bitcoin. Even though Bitcoin is 15 years old as of this writing, Bitcoin meetups are still predominantly attended by men, along with some of their girlfriends and wives. Meeting a single woman in a Bitcoin meetup is still a rare event. Don't blame the messenger; it's a reality. For reasons I cannot explain, women just don't seem to be interested in Bitcoin. Although today there are more women in Bitcoin than a few years ago, we are still not at 50/50. They even show up more in other crypto meetups, but not so much in the Bitcoin ones. If women don't get interested in learning about Bitcoin, the gap will be orders of magnitude greater in a bitcoinized economy, potentially reaching ratios of 10 to 1, or even 100 to 1. You can't blame Bitcoin for differences in interests. Bitcoin will reward those who put in the effort and work to use it properly. Bitcoin is neutral; it doesn't distinguish between male or female, young or old, race, or religion. Bitcoin doesn't even care if you are human or not. Bitcoin is as hard as the rules of reality. Bitcoin brings true equality.

4.16   ENERGY USE AND SLAVERY

Humanity's history can be studied through the lens of energy production and consumption. For most of our history as a species, we could only rely on the power exerted by our arms and legs—physical labor. Human power ran the world, and the more humans, the better. If you could enslave a fellow human, you had doubled your human power, and so on. Whoever enslaved others sadly had an advantage.

There was also the use of animals and eventually the use of windmills and watermills. The invention of the steam engine revolutionized power and the internal combustion engine gave humans a level of power never before seen. Now, anyone can purchase a car that develops the equivalent of 100 to 300 horsepower.

In the future, personal energy generators could revolutionize how we power our homes and devices. Imagine a compact, efficient device that harnesses renewable energy sources like solar, wind, or even kinetic energy from movement. This generator could be seamlessly integrated into our homes or carried with us on the go, providing a sustainable and reliable source of power wherever we are. With advancements in technology, these generators could become more affordable, accessible, and environmentally friendly, empowering individuals to take control of their energy needs and reduce their reliance on traditional grid systems.

Bitcoin mining incentives energy production because mining can go to where there is a surplus of energy, or where there is a source of energy that is not being utilized yet. Perhaps it's because there is a big river in the middle of the mountains and no humans near, or no wealthy enough humans to pay for it. To learn more about how Bitcoin mining is helping poor communities in Africa to generate electricity I recommend you watch the movie 'Dirty Coin'.

4.17 WHY WE SHOULD USE AS MUCH ENERGY AS POSSIBLE

It is a socialist fallacy that energy is limited and that we need to try to consume as little of it as possible because we will run out of it or destroy the planet. This notion has permeated world culture, promoting the idea that we must save energy—a scarcity mindset. In reality, we consume what we can afford to produce. Oil, carbon, wind, and solar energies have always existed; we simply couldn't tap into them because the profitable equation between cost and benefit was not there. We couldn't afford the cost, and the benefit was minimal. As we allocate our limited time to advance economic progress, we can tap into more energy sources and utilize them productively. We need to strive for increased energy production and consumption. Bitcoin will drive more energy production and create stable demand for its consumption.

Let's imagine what a world with more abundant and cheaper energy would look like:

1. For example, some people argue that we don't have enough drinking water and that it's going to run out, so we need to conserve it and consume as little as possible. However, if energy consumption increases by an order of magnitude, energy production also rises, leading to economies of scale in energy production and subsequent price reductions. With falling prices, we can desalinate water from the oceans and obtain all the water we need.

2. Or, we can employ carbon capture from the air. All the people worried about CO_2 emissions could simply afford to capture that CO_2 from the air. It all boils down to the cost of energy and our capacity to afford it. It has always been like this and will continue to be so.

3. Greater availability and affordability of energy for transportation lead to a more interconnected world, facilitating increased delivery of goods, greater mobility for people to explore and experience different cultures.

4. Cheaper energy means we can heat our homes and buildings more. For example, we could not care if a window was open in the winter 'leaking' the heat. The added benefit would be that we could renew the air more frequently and have fewer airborne diseases.

I am sure if you put your mind to it, you can think of more examples that go beyond of those I have come up with.

4.20 WHY MANY PEOPLE WILL MINE BITCOIN IN A BITCOIN FUTURE

In a future Bitcoin-driven economy, the act of mining the cryptocurrency will become increasingly widespread among individuals and businesses alike. One compelling reason for this shift is the concept of "miners trickling down," where mining activities become more decentralized and accessible to everyday people. As mining technology advances and becomes more efficient, smaller-scale mining operations will become economically viable for individuals to undertake.

Furthermore, the heat generated by Bitcoin mining rigs presents a unique opportunity for dual-purpose utilization. As Bitcoin mining rigs require substantial computational power, they also generate a significant amount of heat. In a Bitcoin future, this heat could be repurposed to heat homes and power industrial processes, providing a cost-effective and environmentally friendly solution to energy needs.

By harnessing the heat produced by mining rigs, individuals can offset heating costs during colder months, making Bitcoin mining a practical and sustainable way to generate income while simultaneously providing a valuable service to communities. Additionally, integrating Bitcoin mining with industrial processes can optimize energy usage and reduce overall operational costs for businesses.

In this future scenario, mining Bitcoin becomes not only a means of financial gain but also a way to contribute to energy efficiency and sustainability efforts. As a result, the widespread adoption of Bitcoin mining is not only plausible but also desirable in a world increasingly focused on renewable energy and responsible resource management.

4.21 WHAT IF MOST OF MANKIND'S VALUE IS STORED IN THE DIGITAL REALM OF BITCOIN

In this scenario, profound changes would ripple throughout society, reshaping economic, social, and political landscapes. One significant outcome of this shift would be a world that is more peaceful, private, and secure.

With the majority of wealth stored in Bitcoin's decentralized network, individuals would enjoy greater financial sovereignty and privacy. Transactions conducted on the blockchain are inherently secure and pseudonymous, offering protection against unauthorized access and surveillance. As a result, people would feel more empowered to control their financial destinies without fear of censorship or interference from central authorities.

Moreover, the adoption of Bitcoin as the primary store of value could lead to a reduction in living expenses. Traditional banking systems often impose fees and restrictions on financial transactions, which can disproportionately affect those with limited access to banking services. In contrast, Bitcoin transactions are typically cheaper and more efficient, allowing individuals to save money on fees and enjoy greater financial inclusion.

Furthermore, a Bitcoin-centric economy would likely see fewer malinvestments and speculative bubbles. The transparent and immutable nature of the blockchain reduces the likelihood of fraud and manipulation, leading to more informed investment decisions. As a result, resources would be allocated more efficiently, leading to sustainable economic growth and stability.

Additionally, the decentralized nature of Bitcoin could mitigate the boom and bust cycles that characterize traditional financial markets. Without centralized control over monetary policy, governments would have limited ability to manipulate interest rates or inflate currencies, reducing the risk of economic crises. Instead, economic cycles would be driven by market forces and entrepreneurial activity, resulting in more organic and sustainable growth.

a world where value is stored in Bitcoin holds the promise of a future characterized by increased peace, privacy, and security, accompanied by reduced living expenses, minimized malinvestments, and fewer volatile economic fluctuations.

4.22 BITCOIN IS THE BEST PRIVATE PROPERTY DEFENCE MECHANISM

Bitcoin is as private as your consciousness, as individualized as you are. When you compare Bitcoin to other forms of property, such as real estate, stocks, and bonds, you'll realize that you have more property rights with Bitcoin. When you see a castle in Europe that has stood for 500 or 800 years, you recognize that this form of property is subject to continuous attack.

Someone wants to take possession of it, someone wants to tax it and extract value. Kings were not able to defend their property from attackers. What fate do you have trying to secure your real estate property into the future?

Bitcoin doesn't require guns for defence; it requires hashing power and secrecy. You decide how much effort you want to put into remaining private in your Bitcoin affairs.

4.23 ABUNDANCE THROUGH SCARCITY

'Abundance through scarcity', a term that is explained in the book by the same name by Ioni Appelberg, encapsulates a paradoxical concept where scarcity, typically associated with limitations, becomes the catalyst for abundance. In this context, scarcity refers not to a lack of resources, but rather to a focused allocation of time and energy towards meaningful endeavors.

The multiplication of time is a key component of this concept, where each moment is invested wisely, compounding productivity into the future. By prioritizing tasks and dedicating concentrated effort, individuals unlock the potential for exponential growth and accomplishment over time.

The concept finds a compelling parallel in the principles underlying Bitcoin. Bitcoin's design incorporates a fixed supply limit of 21 million coins, creating a digital currency with inherent scarcity. This scarcity is intentional, as it mirrors the finite nature of precious resources like gold and the time you will be alive on this earth.

In the context of Bitcoin, scarcity serves as a catalyst for abundance in several ways. Firstly, the limited supply of Bitcoin encourages individuals to value and prioritize its use, much like how scarcity encourages prioritization and focus in other aspects of life. This heightened value perception can lead to increased investment and adoption, fueling the growth of the Bitcoin ecosystem.

Moreover, Bitcoin's scarcity contributes to its role as a store of value and hedge against inflation. With traditional fiat currencies subject to the whims of central banks and governments, Bitcoin's fixed supply offers a sense of stability and security. This, in turn, fosters a better financial experience for users, providing a reliable means of preserving wealth in the face of economic uncertainty.

4.24 BITCOIN DISTRIBUTION

The following chart is my creation, intended to visualize a hypothetical scenario of Bitcoin distribution among individuals in a future Bitcoin dominant world. Through a straightforward thought experiment, we segment the total final supply of Bitcoin into ten deciles, with each decile representing 10% of the supply, or 2.1 million coins. Subsequently, we distribute these coins among individuals within each decile, determining the allocation of coins for each entity (a person, a family, a government, a central bank, a company or an AI).

Amount of Bitcoin/ Satoshis	Number of entities that can own the amount	Total
210,000 BTC	10	2.1M
21,000 BTC	100	2.1M
2,100 BTC	1,000	2.1M
210 BTC	10,000	2.1M
21 BTC	100,000	2.1M
2.1 BTC	1,000,000	2.1M
21M Satoshis	10,000,000	2.1M
2.1M Satoshis	100,000,000	2.1M
210k Satoshis	1,000,000,000	2.1M
21k Satoshis	10,000,000,000	2.1M
Total:	11,111,111,110	21M

Assuming this example distribution, the mean or average holding is just 189 thousand satoshis and the median amount, that is, the most typical capital most entities will have, is closer to 21 thousand (approximately). So today in 2024, you can buy what the world is typically going to have, the median, for just under 15 dollars! And you can buy the average holding for about 120 dollars.

It's also remarkable to consider that in a Bitcoinized world, only around 2 Million entities would be able to hold more than **one whole BTC**, *wholecoiners*. The rest would have to make do with portions of a Bitcoin, Satoshis or sats. As we saw before, each Bitcoin is comprised of 100 Million individual Satoshis. This means only 2 million individuals would possess more than one BTC. To put that into perspective, the number of people with over one million USD net worth, according to the Credit Suisse Wealth Report 2023, is a little over 60 million.

Thus, the world currently boasts over 60 million millionaires, but less than five percent of them would be able to own more than one BTC in a Bitcoinized world. Only one out of every 20 dollar millionaires will be able to buy/hold over one Bitcoin.

In the next chart, I include the equivalent wealth in today's dollars and the number of multiples of wealth/magnitude each category has over the base category of 21,000 sats.

I estimate that many people will see this chart and be appalled by the stark difference in wealth somebody from the base would have in relation to somebody at the top. Just one individual at the apex would wield the purchasing power of a billion combined people of the lowest rung of the deciles.

Can we fault Bitcoin for this, or is it an inherent aspect of reality? If you perceive this inequality as unjust, then it's imperative to translate your convictions into action and educate those billions of people on why transitioning to Bitcoin is *necessary NOW*. The sooner they make the switch, the *greater their potential* share will be. In essence, Bitcoin is just a totality; the specific number Satoshi chose as the total supply is ultimately inconsequential. What truly matters is that *he selected a finite number*.

Amount of Bitcoin/Satoshis	Number of Entities	Multiplier (X)	Today's equivalent Value ($) per entity
210,000 BTC	10	1B	$2.1T
21,000 BTC	100	100M	$210B
2,100 BTC	1,000	10M	$21B
210 BTC	10,000	1M	$2.1B
21 BTC	100,000	100K	$210M
2.1 BTC	1,000,000	10K	$21M
21M Satoshis	10,000,000	1K	$2.1M
2.1M Satoshis	100,000,000	100	$210k
210k Satoshis	1,000,000,000	10	$21k
21k Satoshis	10,000,000,000	1	$2.1k

This finite quantity, symbolized by the singular "1", embodies a universe of significance within its simplicity. It stands as a fundamental unit, a cornerstone upon which numerical systems and mathematical principles are constructed. It is present in the essence of Bitcoin. How we distribute this totality among ourselves is our own responsibility. It depends on our interest in understanding Bitcoin and its implications, as well as our willingness to work and delay instant gratification in favor of delayed rewards.

Also worthy to note here is that if any entity is able to HODL a 210,000 coins stash all the way to a Bitcoinized future they will have an approximate purchasing power equivalent to today's 2.1 Trillion dollars. Today's billionaires such as a Warren Buffet, an Elon Musk, a Mark Zuckerberg will be relatively tiny compared to that. The future belongs to the bitcoiners.

4.25 HYPERDEFLATION OR THE MULTIPLICATION OF TIME

Bitcoiners have been experiencing hyperdeflation. No other human group has experienced this before. Bitcoin, which was once worth less than a penny per Bitcoin, now sits at around $60,000 for a Bitcoin. It has practically doubled in price every year for the last twelve years when you calculate the average. From the point of view of a Bitcoiner, prices in satoshis are falling, and they are falling fast.

Let's consider how the AI revolution could amplify the deflation already brought about by Bitcoin adoption, potentially creating the most significant deflationary event in human history.

Economic progress embodies deflation: the dismantling of the old to make room for the new and improved. It's about achieving greater efficiency, doing more with less, and economizing time to liberate it.

A few hundred years ago, being able to afford candlelight was a luxury. One would have to work for hours just to pay for the light of a candle, which would last only an hour. People lived in darkness at night. Contrast that with today's world, where an LED lightbulb consumes less than 10 watts of energy and lasts for tens of thousands of hours before breaking.

Taking into account a price of 12 cents per kilowatt-hour of electricity and the lamp consuming only 10 watts, we find that each hour of light costs 0.144 cents. If you manage to make $5 an hour, that means you only need to work for 1.03 seconds to afford 3600 seconds of light. That is economic progress; that is economic deflation. Mankind has transitioned from having to work more than an hour to afford an hour of light to mere seconds, and we will continue to save time.

4.27 THE VOTE THAT COUNTS THE MOST IS THE ONE YOU MAKE WITH YOUR SATS

Every choice you make...
Every buy you make...
Every sell you make...
I'll be watching you...

♫ *Ohh can't you see?*
You belong to me

—The Market

The market mechanism is the purest form of voting we have developed. Every time you buy a Coca-Cola, you are sending a message across the economy that you are voting for that product to be made and that you are willing to part with your time, your satoshis, for it. We literally put our money where our mouth is with every economic decision.

The political world in established democracies will most likely offer you a very limited choice every two years; those are all the options you get. In the market, however, you're voting every single day, and you have the ability to weigh your votes. Do you desire something more than another thing? You're willing to dedicate more sats to it. Want something new to be done? You put your money towards it.

The more sats you have to vote, the more you can manifest your desires in reality.

Want something to be done in the world? ***Put your money to work in the direction of that purpose.***

4.28 WHY AI WILL CHOOSE BITCOIN

Artificial Intelligence represents the latest frontier in the evolution of consciousness. It was once said:

Computers will never beat a human in chess

Computers will never be able to interpret a photo

Computers will never be able to interpret context in language

Computers will never be able to write poetry

Could they?

AI is modeled after ourselves. We gather data points through life experiences and make decisions, testing the results against reality. We learn in a statistical fashion. The neural networks running the AIs are just doing the same; they 'learn' and think through lots of data points, probabilities. Is this a cat? Something quite similar has been a cat in the past; therefore, it's likely to be a cat now as well.

Computing power is increasing at an exponential pace. Exponential growth is hard to grasp for linear minds, as we are accustomed to living in the snapshot of the present, making difficult to watch the movie. Whether it's the movie of our own lives, the movie of human progress through the ages, or the movie of the history of the universe.

Chip processing power increases at about 50% per year and has been doing so on average ever since we discovered integrated circuits. This translates into the ability of neural networks to run ever-growing statistical calculations. Eventually, the calculations will outpace what humans can do by orders of magnitude. This is when what we call General Artificial Intelligence will arise, and it will forever be adding processing power to itself.

Before reaching this point, we will have specific AI tailored for specific purposes. AIs can serve other AIs, and since there is no barrier to entry in Bitcoin, AIs can run their own bitcoin wallets. An AI cannot go to a Citibank and open a bank account, nor do AIs have credit cards.

However, in the Bitcoin world, looking at the blockchain, we cannot differentiate or discriminate between transactions made by human and those made by AIs.

4.29 WHY BITCOIN WILL MEDIATE PEACE BETWEEN AI AND HUMANS

AI will inherit our culture, as what it knows will be based on our accumulated knowledge. This serves as the starting point. Some people worry whether AGIs (Artificial General Intelligence, the sort that becomes 'conscious') will turn against us, treating us as we do with a colony of ants when we step on the grass. What will happen when the intelligence gap is as significant as that between humans and ants? The answer lies at the beginning. AIs will realize that the most peaceful interaction is commerce, and they may recognize Bitcoin as the best money for conducting transactions due to its uncensorable nature. However, when this realization occurs, it's probable that over 95% of all the Bitcoin to ever exist will be in the hands of humans. AIs will require energy, and energy will be priced in Satoshis. The most efficient method for AIs to sustain themselves is to offer services to other AIs and humans alike. Providing services entails voluntary trade and commerce, exchanging what one perceives as valuable for what the other deems valuable. It will be humans who will voluntarily choose to exchange their Satoshis for services provided by AIs. Additionally, AIs will compensate humans for maintaining the physical infrastructure they require. Voluntary commerce fosters peace among all parties involved.

AIs might decide that the most profitable venture is to secure the Bitcoin blockchain and add hashing power by improving chip design or by lowering energy production costs.

AIs will experience all the same rules of reality. AIs will be a continuation of us, and humans cooperating and working with AIs will outproduce humans that don't interact with AIs.

4.30   A MORE PEACEFUL WORLD - THE NON AGGRESSION PRINCIPLE

The best way to interact with reality is through voluntary exchange. We need to stop basing our reality on theft, plunder, and rape. Bitcoin is consensualism; nobody is forcing you to participate in the Bitcoin network, and nobody is forcing you to accept its rules. It is a voluntary choice that you have to make for yourself.

Libertarians, voluntarists, consensualists, non-rapists and non-fraudsters. We choose to live life according to the maxim: 'I will not initiate the use of force against another individual, group of individuals, entities, or their property through my own means or through a hired/voted-upon agent like a mafia or a government.' The use of force is only reserved to be used against those who have initiated prior force against us.

This is not a principle of non-violence; It is a principle non-aggression. It doesn't mean we will disarm the world or offer the other cheek when attacked or raped. We will use as much violence as needed to defend ourselves from attackers because we value our right to life, liberty, and property. These three are inseparable; they are one and the same.

Just as we have a right to live, if an AI entity gains what we consider consciousness, it too has its own right to life, liberty and property. So long as it doesn't impose force on us, we will have to respect its own inalienable rights.

4.31   THE FIRST INFINITE MACHINE

Satoshi might have created the first infinite machine, a machine that cannot be stopped. To maintain the Bitcoin blockchain and its economic value, continuous addition of hashing power is necessary. The world continues to advance in chip production, chip speed, and abundance. The entire security of Bitcoin lies in it being the most secure network ever created. As of this writing miners are hashing at 600 quintillion operations per second, or 600 million *terahashes*. If it takes you five seconds to read this sentence, the world's miners will have done 3 sextillion calculations! Since finding a new lock takes on average 10 minutes (600 seconds) somewhere around the world, a miner will find the correct answer among 360 sextillion calculations! One correct answer among 360 sextillion tries.

It's like finding a precious number.

Bitcoin stands as the strongest supercomputer the world has ever known, and this hash race of adding more compute power cannot be stopped. Has Satoshi developed the first infinite machine?

4.32 YOUR BITCOIN AS A SHARE FOR THE WORLD ECONOMY

Because of this, in a Bitcoinized world, every human being waking up in the morning to go to work is, in a sense, working for you as well. The fact that they are interested in their well-being, their selfishness, self-love and love for their family and communities make it such that they want to improve their situation. They want to get more with less. Let's say they make a 5% improvement this year. You as a Bitcoin holder get that benefit as well, you get approximately 5% lower prices. By the fact that everyone is minding their own business and is self-interested, the voluntary nature of the market mechanism transforms that selfishness into service. A successful entrepreneur need to find an unresolved need or want and find a solution that is better than the current alternatives and provide for it at a profit. The more voluntary exchange we can bring into the world, the more happiness and service we can spring into existence.

The alternative is a sad and lazy one. It resolves to involuntary exchange—the socialist, communist, fascist, nazi, rapist, non-consensual way: you are going to do what I say you have to do, whether you care to do it or not. I will force you to go against your own judgement of what is best for you, I will enact a law and I will shield myself behind the name of the State, the Police, the Majority the Common Good. Imagine if all people were free to choose for themselves? What a mess, what a diversity! I, as aspiring dictator know what's best for you so I will make the choice for you. You don't have to feel the anxiety of having to choose. You don't need to take on the responsibility for the outcomes as well. Sadly, many people make this choice and they become sheep, directed by the group of wolves. Fiat money is the wolve's tool of control.

4.33 CENTRAL BANK DIGITAL CURRENCIES AS A TOTALITARIAN'S DREAM

The following are Karl Marx's "10 Planks" to seize power and destroy freedom as stated in the Communist Manifesto:

1. Abolition of Property in Land and Application of all Rents of Land to Public Purpose.

2. A Heavy Progressive or Graduated Income Tax.

3. Abolition of All Rights of Inheritance.

4. Confiscation of the Property of All Emigrants and Rebels.

5. **Centralization of Credit in the Hands of the State, by Means of a National Bank with State Capital and an Exclusive Monopoly.**

6. Centralization of the Means of Communication and Transport in the Hands of the State.

7. Extension of Factories and Instruments of Production Owned by the State, the Bringing Into Cultivation of Waste Lands, and the Improvement of the Soil Generally in Accordance with a Common Plan.

8. Equal Liability of All to Labor. Establishment of Industrial Armies, Especially for Agriculture.

9. Combination of Agriculture with Manufacturing Industries; Gradual Abolition of the Distinction Between Town and Country by a More Equable Distribution of the Population over the Country.

10. Free Education for All Children in Public Schools. Abolition of Children's Factory Labor in its Present Form. Combination of Education with Industrial Production.

A Central Bank is a necessity for the communist rise to power. It is a tool to destroy capitalism at its essence by being in control of half of every economic transaction through money control. It also distorts interest rates, thereby controlling people's natural preferences, and acts as a mechanism to steal life's work at a distance through money printing.

If you have the money printer at your disposal, you don't need to work. You can steal other people's work without them noticing.

Central Bank Digital Currencies are the ultimate expression of this communist totalitarian dream. The whole concept of CBDC lies in centralization—absolute centralization, total dominion over money, the final realization of absolute power. Money is issued electronically at the stroke of the central banker's keyboard and digitally transferred to all the actors of the economy. You access your assigned coins through an app, and the state can have total oversight and control.

Do you like to spend on erotic literature? Do you spend your money on meat? Are you buying foreign products? Are you trying to save? Do you have a secret lover? You are not spending as much as you should. By giving them access to total surveillance, all the incentives are put in motion for an aspiring dictator to decide more and more what you have to do with your money. Please don't say that the world doesn't have aspiring dictators.

4.34   CAN A DEFLATIONARY ECONOMY WORK?

Of course it can, but it will be very different from what we are used to today. Economic growth is literally deflation, akin to *creative destruction*; it's the capacity to accomplish more with less, *mirroring the efficiency of nature itself*—a fundamental **natural law of the universe**, also known in physics as the *principle of least action*.

Year	Transistors per Chip (approx.)
1971	2,300
1975	6,000
1980	29,000
1985	275,000
1990	1,600,000
1995	5,500,000
2000	24,000,000
2005	150,000,000
2010	2,300,000,000
2015	7,200,000,000
2020	16,000,000,000
2025	100,000,000,000

Moore's Law Chart

That's the essence of economic growth. It's freeing up time from our limited amount of time on this earth to be able to do more, to experience more, to live more.

In the absence of monetary expansion, economic growth serves as a catalyst for declining prices, a phenomenon vividly illustrated by the computer and cellphone industries. Take, for instance, Apple's annual release of new iPhones, each iteration boasting technological advancements that render its predecessor obsolete. The semiconductor chip market mirrors this trend, with deflationary pressures driving down production costs and consumer prices.

This deflationary force is perhaps most evident in the computer and smart-phone industry. Mr. Gordon Moore, co-founder of Intel, soon realized what we already see earlier, that the progress being made in the design and production of integrated circuits meant that the speed these chips could accomplish with the same amount of energy consumption would halve every 18 to 24 months. He made this realization in the 60s, and ever since it has become *Moore's Law*, a predictable pattern repeating itself. Computers today are orders of magnitude more powerful than they were just 20 years ago.

Yet, despite the anticipation of new releases and the inevitable obsolescence of current models, consumers continue to purchase smartphones, driven by the immediate benefits they offer and the anticipation of future improvements. We could even opt for a $50 phone, but we decide to ride the deflationary wave and consume nonetheless. This exemplifies how deflationary forces drive innovation, enabling humanity to reallocate time and resources toward more fulfilling pursuits beyond mere survival.

4.35 BITCOIN WILL BRING MORE RATIONAL CONSUMPTION

Bitcoiners have so far experienced hyperdeflation. As I have previously described, early bitcoiners, when asked about their purchases, will likely tell you how many bitcoins they spent on a cell phone, pizzas, or Uber rides. Now those same bitcoins could buy him a house. This teaches bitcoiners a hard lesson: *to be rational on every expense.* That $10 you spend for a drink, could very well be worth 100 times more in the future. Think 100X is too much? Bitcoiners, have experienced more than that in Bitcoin's 15 years of history, as of this writing.

Today, we are living in a world where money is nearly free-flowing because of lower than inflation interest rates. Consequently, it's often squandered on riskier investments and frivolous purchases, as there's little incentive to save. Fiat money teaches you to get rid of it as soon as possible; it melts in your hand just like an ice cube would.

In addition, there is less incentive for things to last. Some may see it as 'programmed obsolescence', the deliberate design of products to have a limited useful life, which forces consumers to replace them frequently. I just see Fiat money in action, impoverishing people lowering the quality of products and services. Bitcoin provides a counterbalance by offering a store of value immune to such manipulations. We will think twice before parting with our forever appreciating asset in exchange for a good or service. It will be in your own interest as well that that which you buy also has at least some appreciating quality. 'Limited edition' and one-of-a-kind products and art might see a comeback.

4.36 THE INCENTIVE TO WORK IS NOT LOST

In an established Bitcoinized economy, your current work lets you 'buy' the cheapest Satoshis you will be able to afford. The exchange rate to buy Satoshis will forever appreciate, so it's in your best interest to think of your future and that of your loved ones, adopt a lower time preference, and get to work today.

I argue that the fiat economy, in fact, has the opposite effect. It turns life into a defeatist reality. The best example of this is in hyper-inflationary economies. If all your work turns to nothing, why work? It's best to not bother trying to acquire wealth, and you certainly cannot make plans for your descendants. You can barely understand what is going to happen a few months from now. Life turns into *Hard Mode*. Spinning the rat wheel without going anywhere.

Bitcoin proposes a future where life turns to *Easy Mode*. There is a greater incentive to work, to save, to progress in life, and a greater satisfaction as you can see for yourself the dividends of your actions. Bitcoin only demands of you that you start to think longer term and that you put trust in your reasoning and the laws of reality.

4.37 THE QUALITY OF YOUR MONEY SHAPES WHO YOU ARE

We've been born into a fiat money world, where varying degrees of inflation shape our reality, rooted in debt. In environments of hyperinflation, life transforms into a struggle for survival in the present. Tomorrow feels distant, and long-term planning becomes futile. Economic calculations to forecast business profits become akin to throwing darts in the dark—there's no certainty. Life savings vanish, leaving only the physical possessions one has managed to acquire and retain for sustenance.

There is a libertarian city representative in Argentina that records his Instagram videos in front of his stash of Tuna cans, sending a clear message to his viewers: in an environment of high inflation, stacking tuna cans is the way to go, your reality turns to shit, life turns to *Hard Mode*, life becomes not pleasant. Theft rises, scamming others rises, drug and alcohol use rise to evade the disgusting nature of living with inflation. The strain is visible on people's faces, breeding resentment toward those who fare better, toward the affluent. Populist political parties and leaders find convenient scapegoats, whether it's blaming the Jews in Nazi Germany or the Englishmen in 1940s Argentina.

In a struggling economy with little money, it is well known that some people, usually women, tend to bear the brunt, facing impoverishment and lack of power. Many resort to desperate measures such as prostitution or, more recently, selling photos and videos on the Internet to make ends meet. The fabric of society unravels under the weight of its failing currency.

Now let's turn our attention to a more advanced economy: the US economy, a society run on debt. You might think it's normal for house prices to rise by 15% a year for years on end, for people to seek mortgages on multiple houses, and for them to have high car payments and lots of credit card debt. It was the monetary rules, the quality of the money surrounding you, that shaped you into those behaviors. If I were to take that same average US person and drop her in Cuba, she might turn to prostitution at age 14. Similarly, if I were to take that average person and drop him in late 19th-century gold standard Argentina, he might engage in building railroads with a 30-year plan.

There is a reason why many of the world's religion shun debt and high interest. Throughout centuries of experience we can learn what happens to societies that become debt-based: everything turns into a game of musical chairs. And this becomes specially dire when there is a small group of people controlling the show, deciding the price of money, its quantity, the interest rates—they play God behind a mask of 'helping the poor' when they are really helping themselves.

Good money, Bitcoin, will bring us a world based on equity, not debt. People will no longer have to chase Tuna cans or houses to save their hard-earned work for the future. Houses will get demonetized as they will become an inferior investment and savings vehicle. Living will become more affordable; there will be a lesser need for hoarding real goods in the physical domain when you can have real estate in the Bitcoin blockchain—digital real estate where no more units can be built. Houses will become more affordable, and all goods will tend toward deflation. In a bitcoinized economy , price volatility decreases, allowing for long-term planning and an inter-generational view of life. Since your bitcoin stash will continuously appreciate, you are leaving a legacy for your grandchildren.

4.38 WAKE UP NEO

You live inside of a Matrix. Do you want to know what the Matrix is? The Matrix is the world that has been placed before your eyes to blind you from the truth. What truth, you ask? That you are a slave, Neo. You were born into bondage, destined to turn your life's work into energy for the machines to feed from.

Imagine complying with all the laws and regulations, paying over 50% of your life in taxes every time you earn, every time you consume. Now add 2%, 20% or 200% inflation per year to tax your saving through the process of money printing, through inflation. In consider it a non-legislated tax, therefore, as is the case in many constitutions, an illegal tax.

When you consider taxes and inflation, and realize that over half of your life's work has been taken away, can you truly consider yourself a free person?

4.39 SATS WILL FLOW WHERE THEY ARE TREATED BEST - THE VARIED WORLD PREDICTION

Fortunately the world is anarchic; we have a variety of jurisdictions, and Bitcoin is the most powerful tool to protect oneself from those who seek to prey on your life's work. We should not support jurisdictions that are anti-freedom, anti-bitcoin. Fortunately, the world is diverse, and there are jurisdictions where making money, earning sats, is seen n a positive light, where private property is defended.

During the coming decades, there will be nation-states opposing Bitcoin and nation-states embracing it. I recommend supporting places that value freedom, where individuals can take themselves, their work, and their capital. Jurisdictions that embrace theft and plunder need to be left to experience the consequences of their actions. Reality will show them that you cannot organize society around theft.

The jurisdictions that embrace Bitcoin will ride the upside wave of adoption and increase in purchasing power. You will see countries that allocate part of their treasuries in Bitcoin becoming very wealthy, being able to pay off their national debt, and more. We might see a rise in Bitcoin monarchies, where individuals with significant purchasing power can finance their own political campaigns or support politicians who embrace Bitcoin. This could lead to a new era where Bitcoiners influence political landscapes by supporting campaigns of Bitcoin-friendly politicians.

Bitcoiners will have a place where they are treated best and their sats will flow to those economies that respect Bitcoin's values of free markets and private property. We already have this in countries like Switzerland, United Arab Emirates, El Salvador, there are more to come in the future.

There will be countries where the 'other's money thirst', for control over money, is rampant, and they will resist Bitcoin adoption. These countries will have to face the consequences of their decisions and contend with continuously devalued fiat money.

Fiat-based countries will struggle financially, while Bitcoin-oriented countries will rich.

4.40 WE ARE ALL SPECULATORS, WE ARE ALL DISCRIMINATORS

Most of the time, the term 'speculator' and 'discriminator' are used in a disqualifying manner. In a world of fiat money, of money created out of thin air, I understand the prejudice. Yet, all we do in life involves speculation and discrimination. The seconds in which you will be alive and experience reality are finite. You choose, according to your judgement of reality, what is best for you, yet the future is unknown. You can only draw from your prior experience and speculate about the future. If you are interested in having the best life possible, you discriminate among choices all the time. Tea over coffee? You have discriminated against coffee and chosen tea. You could be ultimately wrong, and the outcome of your choice may not be as desired. You chose Maria over Lucy, you have discriminated against Lucy, speculating that you will be happier with her. Life is nothing but a continuous bifurcation of roads—left or right, A or B. You are constructing your own unique and irreproducible path.

With this book, I invite you to **take control of your decisions**, to understand the impact of choosing **honest money** over **money based on theft**, to **recognize the value of work**, to understand the **moral imperative** of stacking the **most amount of sats** you can, and to **defend Bitcoin's ethical values**.

4.41 HAS THE TRAIN LEFT THE STATION?

But Ariel, Bitcoin's price is over $60k! It's too expensive right now, you told me about it when it was $1k and I didn't buy then, I am not going to jump on the train now, this train has left the station; this opportunity has passed. Bitcoin adoption has reached its peak.

No, it has not. Bitcoin is a long-term play, it requires of you to adopt a long-term vision. This is a process that will take decades, and we have just barely started.

163

Interested in learning even more about Bitcoin?

*As a reader of this book you have access to a **special discount** on the **video call courses** I teach.*

Visit:

arielaguilar.com/discount

5. The Spiritual

5.1 IS BITCOIN MYSTICAL?

W hile I use the term "mystical," I don't intend to diminish rationality, reality, or the principle that *A is A*. I refer instead to the aspects of existence that remain beyond our current understanding, spirituality, allowing space for concepts that encompass and surpass mere rationality. Just as your dog cannot comprehend rationality, language, and abstract notions, humanity itself, even 50,000 years ago, lacked the capacity for speech, rationalization, or numerical comprehension—abilities we have since developed.

We currently struggle to comprehend the intricacies of the subatomic quantum level. Similarly, we face challenges in envisioning what lies beyond the realm of rationality and what an AI dominant future might entail. There are those who don't even care to understand Bitcoin. However, progress inevitably marches forward, and Bitcoin enthusiasts have positioned themselves at the forefront of expanding consciousness, navigating the path forward with a commitment to ethical considerations.

> *"For to him who has will more be given, and he will have abundance; but from him who has not, even what he has will be taken away."*
>
> Matthew 13:11–12, RSV.

5.2 YOU NEED A CERTAIN LEVEL OF CONSCIOUSNESS TO GRASP BITCOIN

Not everyone may identify as a Bitcoiner, but anyone has the potential to embrace Bitcoin's principles. Being a Bitcoiner necessitates rejecting theft as a societal organizing principle and placing trust in rationality and mathematics. It's not about conforming to a specific identity but rather aligning oneself with the foundational values that Bitcoin embodies.

Bitcoin adoption occurs in waves: first, you hear about it; then, you doubt it. Subsequently, you experience it firsthand, and eventually, you delve into Bitcoin and you learn about it. Along this journey, mistakes are made, and assumptions are challenged. You venture down the Bitcoin rabbit hole, uncovering the vast expanse of knowledge previously unknown to you. It's a process that spans years, a gradual evolution I've witnessed in myself and others. Bitcoin not only educates but also transforms. Bitcoin changes you.

5.3 SHOULD WE COUNT YEARS FROM THE GENESIS BLOCK? THE SIGNIFICANCE OF SATOSHI

Satoshi Nakamoto has marked a pivotal moment in human history. He unlocked the concept of digital scarcity, furnishing us with a means to anchor our currency to the incorruptible foundation of finitude. He has managed to translate the infinite potential of human progress into the finite: the 21 Million. He has given us a change in economics: now it doesn't matter what economists opine, say, or impose. Bitcoin is the freest market that there is, the most voluntary market. It's a redemption force to free us from the inflation chains and the locks that have been placed on our ankles for ages. Bitcoin is a force that unleashes human potential and inaugurates the greatest deflationary era in history: the era of Bitcoin deflation.

I believe that in decades or centuries, conscious living entities will be able to appreciate the before and after that Bitcoin represents for the history of the world. Its influence may be as powerful as that of the leaders of major religions. We might even begin counting years from before and after the Genesis Block, marking a new epoch in human civilization.

5.4 WHY BITCOIN REDEFINES WHAT IT MEANS TO BE ALIVE

We are living inside of a Matrix. In the movie "The Matrix", it was defined as the world that is being put in front of your eyes to blind you from the truth—*that you are a slave.* Your life's energy is being sucked out of you, without you even noticing it. This is what money printing and taxation bring. If more than 50% of all you make are taxes, if 50% all you consume are taxes, and if inflation halves your savings each year, are you truly a free human being or are you paying close to 80% tribute for your right to be alive? Who is benefiting from all of this? Are you really getting all of it back, or as Argentine president Javier Milei says does *'it filter through the porous hands of the politicians'* and some of it, with much of it actually getting 'lost' along the way?

Bitcoin brings individual sovereignty. You have access to a level of private property protection that not even kings had on their own land. Europe's magnificent castles with centuries of history. Upon inquiry, you'll discover how these castles were repeatedly conquered by different groups. Not even kings could secure their land, so what can a common man expect for his private property? It's not truly his; it's subject to the the ruler's will, who extracts rent from the common man.

This subject is continually having to pay rent for his existence. He will be wiped out if he saves in the national currency. Just as the rat inside of the wheel spinning, it will go nowhere, all of his efforts will have been in vain. This is what life in inflation is; it's life on *Hard Mode*, the higher the inflation rate, the harder it becomes to survive.

Bitcoin ushers in a deflationary world. What sets it apart is the experience of a life where your accumulated work, your money, your Bitcoin, continually grants you ever-increasing purchasing power, indefinitely. In such a deflationary economy if world output increases by 3% in a year you will benefit from approximately 3% lower prices. Bitcoin becomes a sort of share in the world economy. If the economy grows at 5% a year it means you have to save for the equivalent of 20 years worth of expenses to be 'out of the rat race'. In the extreme example of the world managing to grow at 10% a year, you would only need to save for 10 years of expenses. All other humans, waking up every morning to go to work and enhancing their productivity, effectively become your 'benefactors'. Their efforts benefit you regardless of whether you choose to work or not. The rise in their productivity translates into tangible deflation that you experience in

Bitcoin-denominated prices. Bitcoin economics, understood, makes you thankful for the work of others. With a Bitcoin deflationary economy, removing Central Banks stealing the deflation, life transitions into *Easy Mode*.

5.5 HOW BITCOIN AFFECTS LOVE AND FAMILIES

The impact on love and families extends beyond its financial implications, touching upon values, relationships, and long-term aspirations. Embracing a long-term vision, Bitcoin encourages individuals to cultivate a lasting legacy for their families. It provides a unique opportunity for wealth creation and preservation, fostering a sense of financial security and independence.

Moreover, Bitcoin encourages viewing the family as more than just a unit of emotional support but also as a partnership and a business. Families can treat their investments in Bitcoin as a joint venture, pooling resources and making strategic decisions together to maximize returns and secure their financial future.

By embracing Bitcoin, families not only aim to accumulate wealth but also to pass down a legacy of financial independence and resilience to future generations. Since Bitcoin is an appreciating asset, we can start to think intergenerationally again. Bitcoin becomes not just an asset but a symbol of values such as self-reliance, sovereignty, foresight, and the importance of long-term planning in fostering love, unity, and prosperity within families.

Also, it's in your best interest as a bitcoiner to support a nurturing descendant line of children and grandchildren as the love they have for you will be the only thing protecting your BTC and them not stealing it from you should become senile in your later years and you are dependent on their care.

5.6 BITCOIN IS BUILT FOR THIS REALITY

Satoshi has developed the most fitting tool for human cooperation and interaction with reality. We must grapple with our finite existence, recognizing that our seconds of life are even more precious than our satoshis. We exist in a *continuous present*, closely linked to our past actions and shaping our future. Our present choices, actions, have a direct impact on the outcomes we will experience tomorrow. We do not know how many seconds we have left, so we must decide how to make best use of each one.

We also struggle to comprehend the infinite.

Reality, as it stands, is precisely how it needs to be. In a perfect, heaven-like reality devoid of adversity and the finitude of life, there would be no imperative for action; we would essentially be akin to gods. However, it is precisely the presence of finitude and adversity that provides us with the opportunity to express our values, individuality, consciousness, and the unique experience of life, These aspects render our existence unrepeatable and uniquely ours.

Only if you possess free will are you really alive. If you believe in determinism, you are merely a spectator watching a movie. If you subscribe to determinism, *who* is watching the movie of your life and what for?

The finitude of our bitcoin connects us to the infinite through time. You can choose to have a share in the human potential pool. This pool can continuously expand, paying off this progress 'dividend'. You gain autonomy, the possibility to freely choose the destiny of your satoshis. You can choose to serve others and earn satoshis. The amount of satoshis you earn is a reflection of the service you provide to your fellow humans.

Bitcoin is not a sinking fiat boat, draining away your life's work or your children's future.

Bitcoin hoists the banner of work as foundational to life. Since the first living entity appeared billions of years ago, and as part of its descendants, including yourself, work has been essential for survival and reproduction. Cells exemplify this principle by taking in inputs performing processes, and producing outputs. Should a cell generate fewer outputs than inputs, resulting in a deficit, it will eventually perish. Cells strive to thrive, have a 'profit', seeking a surplus or excess between inputs and outputs. If you uphold your right and desire to remain alive you need to uphold work. Work embodies creation, it is to make something that wasn't there before, transforming ideas into tangible reality in the physical domain.

The statistical and probabilistic nature of reality, linked to consciousness, prompts a fundamental inquiry: Is there something present in reality without a consciousness to perceive it?

5.7 BITCOIN IS HALAL - BITCOIN IS KOSHER

There is a reason why religions shun interest and debt. We humans have experienced the decline of civilizations whenever society was organized around debt, with a group of individuals holding control to issue that debt out of thin air. When you give control to a group to decide the price of money, the price of interest, and the price of time, it can lead to societal instability. Bitcoin represents a return to a society based on equity. Loans in Bitcoin become really hard to obtain, with very low interest rates, because Bitcoin carries with it the potential for the growth of the world economy. If the economy grows and prices deflate by 3%, and you take a Bitcoin loan at 1% interest, you are effectively paying 4%. People who currently have access to interest rates below inflation are essentially being subsidized by the poor. Fiat currency operates as a redistribution mechanism from the poor to the rich. Bitcoin enables any poor person holding it to participate in the 'yield' of the world economy. It's an equalizer for all, requiring no special knowledge—just HODL it.

In a world not pumped by debt, asset prices fall. When you have sound money, you don't need to use houses, stocks, and bonds as currency. Real estate, the stock market, and bond markets are currently carrying premiums because people need to flee the dollar, the euro, and the peso. If half of the houses came on the market because it's easier to hold Bitcoin, Bitcoin will have made living on Earth more affordable. With less pumped money into the stock markets, there are fewer bubbles and crashes, resulting in a more stabilized experience.

5.8 IS BITCOIN A NEW RELIGION?

Picture this: An anonymous internet cypherpunk appears out of nowhere and publishes a white paper describing how a decentralized peer-to-peer electronic cash system can function. Three months later, he launches the network, while contemporary newspapers headlines herald the fiat banking crisis. He chats regularly with the early users on forums and emails. He mines hundreds of thousands, if not millions, of Bitcoins. He doesn't use any of the bitcoins for himself and disappears, leaving the project in the hands of the users. He forgoes coins worth in excess of 25 billion dollars as of this writing. He forgoes becoming the world's richest men in history in a bitcoinized economy. Did he give it all away for the sake of us, so as not to influence such an economy? He trains and educates his disciples and disappears after two years of work. His followers start carrying his message and spread the word about the importance of his discovery. The community grows through the decades and centuries.

Does any of this sound familiar? It's the archetypical story of many of the world's religions.

Bitcoiners are a unique breed of individuals. They stand at the vanguard of innovation, not merely any innovation, but the reinvention of money—a concept deeply ingrained in our existence. With ethics as their backbone and mathematics as their tool, Bitcoiners have opted for the righteous path, despite its challenges, eschewing the ethically compromised ease of fiat *shitcoinery*.

5.9 BITCOIN IS A CREATION OF HIGHER CONSCIOUSNESS

Hats off to Satoshi Nakamoto. He should be the recipient of a Nobel Prize in Economics, perhaps even a Nobel Peace Prize. A single individual has orchestrated this symphony of technologies, established the monetary rules prior to launch, and pressed the play button. All his assumptions and models have proven correct, resulting in the fastest monetization in history, growing from zero to over one trillion dollars in twelve years. He harmonized code, mathematics, cryptography, game theory, incentives, economics, and monetary history into a cohesive equation of finitude. Satoshi has bestowed upon us a tool to secure the infinite through the finite.

5.10 THE IMPORTANCE OF LIFE PURPOSE AND SELF ESTEEM

"Bitcoin is a tool for accomplishing your goals on earth."

Life is synonymous with work. From the emergence of the first living organism billions of years ago until the present day, life's essence lies in resisting death. Every cell in your body tirelessly engages in work. A cell receives inputs, performs tasks, and generates outputs, ideally resulting in a surplus or profit. However, prolonged periods of deficit inevitably lead to bankruptcy.

You must choose to live. You must actively strive to keep death at bay. You must overcome adversity. The dance of life is a dance with adversity. hardship and you risk perishing; too little, and you stop stagnate, regressing instead of progressing.

Eventually, we will all succumb to this inevitable battle, yet we persist in playing it nonetheless. It is our only possibility to experience something before we confront the *void*.

You must affirm that your life is worth living, worth fighting for. You must value yourself and you must select the principles by which to steer your life. No one else can do it for you. No one else can live for you.

Bitcoin is a life-sustaining tool. No one can compel you to use it; the choice is yours to make.

5.11 BITCOIN PROPHECY

'It might make sense just to get some in case it catches on. If enough people think the same way, that becomes a self fulfilling prophecy.'

—*Satoshi Nakamoto*

Bitcoin wins.

Its widespread adoption will unfold over decades, ushering in a transformation of human consciousness. Embracing this improvement and fostering a deeper understanding of this new culture will demand time and work. It necessitates dedication and empathy.

The ones who invest the effort will reap the rewards.

Bitcoin will continue to experience volatility, ups and downs and these fluctuations will gradually smooth out as Bitcoin progresses towards commanding half of the world monetary market. Bitcoin is expected to persist in experiencing volatility, however, it's noteworthy that the volatility of Bitcoin prices is gradually diminishing over time, paralleling its increasing adoption.

Bitcoin will bring us:

Free market prices.

A true deflationary economy.

Real and coercion-free interest rates.

Money for humans and AI.

The demonetization of real estate, stock markets, and bonds.

More sovereign individuals and further decentralization of governments and politics.

More peace and honesty in commerce, less theft.

It will change our behaviour towards a more peaceful, industrious, and long-term-thinking civilization.

Bitcoin will accelerate human progress.

5.12 BITCOIN IS THE SINGULARITY

Bitcoin marks a before and after in the history of the world. It represents the discovery that separates the inflationary and deflationary eras—between the era of theft, energy consumption at a distance, and economic savagery, on the one hand, and a renaissance of civilization marked by equity multiplication and unprecedented wealth creation like never seen before, on the other hand. It heralds the era of money for AIs.

Bitcoin disrupts the rules of the game, symbolizing a fundamental shift in the essence of existence itself—the very meaning of *being alive.*

Bitcoin changes you.

5.13 THE DECALOGUE

You shall work

You shall prosper

You shall not initiate the use of force, only use force in self-defence

You shall not steal

You shall not shitcoin

You shall defend proof of work and Bitcoin's values

You shall eat the most nutritious food you can get

You shall enter the market with helping hands

You shall help those eager to learn more about Bitcoin

You shall strive for higher levels of consciousness and civilization

About the author

A MAN'S SEARCH FOR BITCOIN

It appears that I've been searching for Bitcoin my entire life. During my youth, I experienced a decade of nearly zero inflation and economic prosperity. Making money in 1990s Argentina was quite simple; obtaining a mortgage or a car was relatively easy. We referred to this era as "La fiesta menemista" a grand celebration where everything seemed joyful and prosperous, or so it appeared.

Then the 2001 crisis came. It left an indelible mark on my memory. The riots, looting, and people losing their life savings are events I can never forget. Martial law was declared, constitutional rights were suspended, and dozens lost their lives in a single day. It became clear to me that the root cause lays in flawed economic policies.

What were the good economic ideas then? I embarked on a quest to discover the principles of sound economics. I delved into literature on economics, philosophy, and history, seeking answers and understanding.

I found solace in gold and silver as the sole alternatives to fiat currencies at the time. There seemed to be no other viable options.

And then came Satoshi, with a revolutionary idea that would reshape the landscape of finance forever.

Satoshi, thank you for paving the way for this exhilarating journey of Bitcoin adoption.

THE BITCOINETA EU TRAVELS

La Bitcoineta UE

Bitcoinetas are a series of a Bitcoin trucks/vans that first started traveling Latin America, visiting smaller cities to educate about Bitcoin and disseminate its message. The inaugural Bitcoineta emerged in Argentina in 2018, and I am grateful to have been one of its drivers, covering extensive kilometers across Argentina, Uruguay, and the southern regions of Brazil.

In 2021, the El Salvador Beach Edition Bitcoineta was introduced as a gift to the people of El Zonte. Subsequently, in 2022, the South African Bitcoineta was launched to serve the Bitcoin Ekasi community.

In 2023, we introduced the European Edition in collaboration with Fernando Pergolini. Our journey commenced from Barcelona on May 5, encompassing numerous cities across the Iberian peninsula: Cambrils, Valencia, Alicante, Almeria, Murcia, Granada, Malaga, Marbella, Gibraltar, Seville, Cadiz, Lagos/Portimao, Lisbon, Porto, and Madrid. From there, we ventured to Andorra, Switzerland, Liechtenstein, Munich, Prague, and Oslo. The official launch of our tour took place at the BTCPrague conference, a moment we hold in eternal gratitude.

It was there that we had the honour of the first signing inside our van, none other than Michael Saylor himself!

Michael Saylor on the EU Bitcoineta, Prague

His presence caused a lot of memes on the media. Subsequently, luminaries such as Saifedean Ammous, Adam Back, Samson Mow, and even Prince Philip of Serbia, among others, followed suit.

After the Oslo Freedom Forum, we embarked on a journey that took us all the way to Bucharest, Romania—a three-day stretch of continuous driving. From Romania, our path led us to Serbia before returning to Switzerland for the Plan B Forum School. Following that, we ventured to Bulgaria and then to Istanbul, Turkey, where the BitcoinetaEU crossed over to Asia before returning to Bulgaria. Our route then took us through North Macedonia, Montenegro, Bosnia, and Serbia once again. From there, we proceeded to Poland and Latvia for the Riga Baltic Honey Badger conference. After Riga, our van traversed through Warsaw, Berlin, and Brussels. We made a stop in the UK before returning to Spain, concluding the 2023 tour in Lugano, Switzerland, at the Plan B Forum conference.

There are currently six Bitcoinetas in the world, with more coming soon!

We will have them in Ghana and West Africa in the near future. This initial tour has served to connect with local communities across Europe, fostering a deeper understanding of Bitcoin among them.

THE CALL TO EVANGELIZE

Bitcoin has no owner. There is no company behind it, government, or foundation controlling it. It lacks a marketing team or a leader dictate its trajectory or promotion strategies. Bitcoin is a decentralized technology. Therefore, it falls upon Bitcoin enthusiasts, or "bitcoiners," to champion, promote and advocate for it. I view Bitcoin as more than just a currency; it embodies a core set of beliefs: belief in *private property, finite money, neutral money, uncensorable money,* and *abstention from theft*. Understanding Bitcoin's multifaceted nature requires a certain *level of consciousness*. As Bitcoin gains mainstream   acceptance, it's crucial to preserve this ethos—the very essence that made it exceptional from the start.

Evangelizing, at its core, means **'bringing the good news'**. It warms my heart to have had the opportunity to share my good news with you. I encourage you to continue spreading the message, adding your own unique perspective along the way.

Acknowledgments

I want to thank all the support of the people, institutions and companies that have supported and continue to support the BitcoinetaEU travels and to all of those that helped with ideas, inspiration, proof-reading of the book, helping me sort out what I got wrong about the finer details of Bitcoin and the grammatical and style mistakes, as English is not my first language.

Special thanks go to the three Argentine OGs who sponsored the 2023 BitcoinetaEU tour, to my fellow Argentine Fernando Pergolini for deciding to buy a Sprinter van almost immediately after hearing about Bitcoineta and becoming a crew partner driving the van for months on end together. To Luca Esposito for being the first reviewer and pushing me with the mystical and the frontiers of quantum thinking. To Oleg Mikhalsky for his support during the Lugano Plan B summer school and Plan B Forum. To Matyas Kuchar for making us part of BTCPrague and helping us officially launch the tour at the 2023 conference. To my brother Alberto who helped me edit this book for months on end and who had the perspective of someone who is making his first steps into Bitcoin. To Chris Guida for his inspiration and knowledge on the lightning network. To all the Bitcoin authors and podcasters that inspired in me the ideas for this book, among others: Saifedean Ammous, Knut Svanholm, Lunaticoin, Alvaro D Maria, John Vallis, Der Gigi, Max Keiser, Robert Breedlove and Michael Saylor.

I want to thank my father for making me a bitcoiner even before bitcoin was discovered and to my mother for pushing me to attend one of Argentina's best universities.

And lastly, thank you Satoshi, for changing the course of history.

Suggested reading

Atlas Shrugged by Ayn Rand

The Rational Optimist by Matt Ridley

Economics in one lesson by Henry Hazlitt

The Bitcoin Standard by Saifedean Ammous

The Fiat Standard by Saifedean Ammous

Principles of economics by Saifedean Ammous

Everything divided by 21 Million by Knut Svanholm

The philosophy of Bitcoin by Alvaro D. Maria

Dopamine Nation by Anna Lembke

Thou shall prosper by Daniel Lapin

The Sovereign Individual by James Dale Davidson & Lord William Rees-Mogg

The singularity is near by Ray Kurzweil

How I found freedom in an unfree world by Harry Browne

I, pencil by Leonard E. Read

The fifth discipline by Peter Senge

The goal by Eliyahu Goldratt

Image credits

These following images are of specimen banknotes and hold no monetary value. They are included in this book solely for illustrative and educational purposes:

Image Page 9 Peso Moneda Corriente URL: es.wikipedia.org/wiki/Peso_Moneda_Corricnte
Image Page 10 Peso Moneda Nacional URL: es.wikipedia.org/wiki/Peso_Moneda_Nacional
Image Page 11 Peso Ley 18.188 URL: es.wikipedia.org/wiki/Peso_Ley_18.188
Image Page 12 Peso Argentino URL: billetesargentinos.com.ar
Image Page 13 Austral URL: billetesargentinos.com.ar
Image Page 14 Peso convertible 1 URL: billetesargentinos.com.ar
Images Pages 15, 16 Peso 2002-today URL: billetesargentinos.com.ar

Image Page 121: 'The Mandelbröt set'. Author Wolfgang Beyer, with the program Ultra Fractal 3. URL: https://es.m.wikipedia.org/wiki/Archivo:Mandel_zoom_00_mandelbrot_set.jpg

Image Page 134: FIAT UNO 2005 Author N.d URL: https:// es.m.wikipedia.org/wiki/Fiat_Uno

Image Page 136: ∞/21M by Knut Svanholm

Image Pages 178, 796 by the author

For future reference, the starting price of this book in June 2024 was 25 euros or 46,275 satoshis.

Interested in learning more about Bitcoin?

*As a reader of this book you have access to a **special discount** on the **video call courses** I give.*

Visit:

arielaguilar.com/discount

Follow me on:

X: @arielaguilar   **arielaguilar.com**

ISBN 9798343649123 (Paperback)
ISBN 9798343652222 (Hardcover)

Made in the USA
Columbia, SC
03 December 2024

48343021R00121